# Marit R. Westergaard

## Definite NP Anaphora: A Pragmatic Approach

# Marit R. Westergaard

# Definite NP Anaphora: A Pragmatic Approach

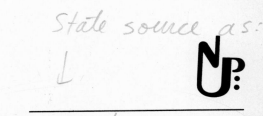

**Norwegian University Press**

Norwegian University Press (Universitetsforlaget AS), 0608 Oslo 6
Distributed World-Wide excluding Scandinavia by
Oxford University Press, Walton Street, Oxford OX2 6DP

London   New York   Toronto
Delhi   Bombay   Calcutta   Madras   Karachi
Kuala Lumpur   Singapore   Hong Kong   Tokyo
Nairobi   Dar es Salaam   Cape Town
Melbourne   Auckland

and associated companies in
Beirut   Berlin   Ibadan   Mexico City   Nicosia

Cover design: Harald Gulli

**British Library Cataloguing in Publication Data**

Westergaard, Marit R.
   Definite NP anaphora: a pragmatic approach
   1. Anaphora (Linguistics)
   I. Title
   415       P299.A5

ISBN 82-00-06950-8

Typeset in Norway by ty'pisk as, Tromsø
Printed in Norway by Nye Intertrykk as, Bærum

# Preface

This thesis is the result of influence from two very different courses. The topic, definite NP anaphora, caught my interest during a syntax course conducted by Professor Sandra Chung at the University of California, San Diego, during the winter quarter of 1984, while the functional framework which forms the foundation of my analysis is essentially that which was introduced to me during a course in pragmatics at the University of Tromsø given by Professor Leiv Egil Breivik in the spring semester of 1982. The thesis was written during the fall semester of 1984 under the supervision of Professor Breivik and submitted to the School of Languages and Literature in partial fulfillment of the requirements for the *cand.philol.* degree in January 1985.

Many of the examples given in this thesis are my own, but many are also modifications of sentences that occur at various places in the existing literature on anaphora. It is thus difficult in each case to identify exactly where the sentence in question originated. I will therefore refer to the source of the examples only in cases of direct quotation.

The thesis consists of six chapters. The first is a presentation of the linguistic phenomenon of pronominal anaphora, while the second is an outline of the previous research that has been done on this topic within the framework of transformational-generative grammar. The third chapter contains a criticism of this purely syntactic approach to anaphora, and in Chapter 4 I proceed to suggest a new solution to the problem of anaphoric relations based on pragmatic principles. Chapter 5 is devoted to the testing of this hypothesis against sentences that frequently occur in the current discussion on anaphora. Chapter 6 constitutes the conclusion and consists mainly of a summary of the theory outlined in this thesis, as well as sections on remaining problems and ideas for further research.

# Contents

# 1
# Introduction

## 1.0 The Phenomenon

Despite the massive amount of literature devoted to linguistic phenomena in English before the arrival of transformational-generative grammar, no explicit attention was paid to the problems related to the coreference options of pronouns and full NPs in sentences like the following:

(1) *Leslie* liked the man who kissed *her.*[1]

(2) **She* liked the man who kissed *Leslie.*[2]

In (1), it is understood that the full NP, *Leslie,* and the pronoun *her* refer to the same individual in the outside world—this is at least what would be assumed when a sentence like this is uttered out of context. For (2) to be acceptable, on the other hand, the pronoun and the full NP must refer to two different individuals. The question, then, which naturally arises from this, is the following: when can a pronoun and a full NP in the same sentence refer to the same entity, and when is it impossible for them to corefer? A satisfactory explanation of this linguistic phenomenon requires several aspects of natural language to be taken into account.

## 1.1 The Transformational-generative Framework

Within more recent linguistic theory, there has been no dearth of research into this aspect of English grammar, now usually discussed as problems of *anaphora.* Especially within the generative framework, important linguists like Lees and Klima (1963), Langacker (1969), Ross (1969), Postal (1971), McCawley (1984), Chomsky (1980, 1981) and Reinhart (1976, 1981, 1983a and b), to mention but a few, have sought to explain this phenomenon on the basis of syntactic structure, represented in the by now so familiar tree diagrams. The syntactic relationship between the full NP and the pronoun has been found to be of great importance for the coreference options of the two elements, and in the present state of the theory this relationship is most commonly defined in terms of the notion *c-command,* which is due to Reinhart (1976).

An impressive amount of interesting facts has been discovered about pronominal anaphora as well as other syntactic phenomena in the course of this research. The pragmatic aspects of pronominal reference have, however, been mainly disregarded by generative grammarians, and are actually claimed to be of no importance for the coreference options available for the NPs of a sentence.

## 1.2    *A Hypothesis*

I would claim, however, that pragmatic facts such as discourse context, theme/rheme relations, information and focus structure may interact with syntactic structure in this respect, and that a theory of pragmatics is required to explain the full range of coreference possibilities of pronouns and full NPs. My hypothesis is that pragmatic structure not only interacts with syntactic structure, but sometimes even interferes with it, and in subsequent chapters I will argue that a functional approach to this problem is needed to solve the still remaining problems of anaphora.

## 1.3    *Aim and Scope*

In this thesis, therefore, I will first give a brief outline of the history and development of the recent linguistic research on pronominal anaphora. I will then discuss some of the problems that arise when a purely syntactic approach is used, and show that syntax alone is not capable of accounting for all the coreference options of pronouns and full NPs. An attempt will then be made to take various pragmatic factors into consideration when analyzing this linguistic phenomenon, and the theory that is postulated will finally be tested and compared with the purely syntactic one.

## 1.4    *The Reflexive and Reciprocal Processes*

The reference options for reflexive and reciprocal pronouns, as illustrated in (3) and (4) below, have traditionally been discussed together with pronominal anaphora. These processes will, however, be disregarded in this thesis, as I consider them to be governed mainly by syntactic factors.

(3)  a.  Leslie's *brother* likes *himself.*
   -    b.*Leslie's* brother likes *herself.*

(4)  a.  *Leslie and Peter* helped *each other.*
       b.*Leslie and Peter* forced the teacher to help *each other.*

Much of the recent literature on the topic of anaphora, especially within the framework of Government and Binding as outlined in Chomsky (1981), has been focused on the relationship between quantified NPs and *wh*-elements on the one hand and pronouns, in these cases interpreted as bound variables, on the other, as for example in the following sentences:

(5)  a.  *Each candidate* thanked the people who voted for *him.*
       b.*He* thanked the people who voted for *each candidate.*

(6)  a.  *Who* thanked the people who voted for him?
       b.*Who did the people who voted for *him* like *t*?[3]

The anaphoric versus non-anaphoric relations of (5) and (6) will not be considered in the present analysis either. Rather, the attention of this thesis will be restricted to the syntactic structures and pragmatic factors governing the coreference options of pronouns and full definite NPs, as illustrated in examples (1) and (2) above.

# 2
# Background

## 2.0 *Introduction*

In this chapter I will briefly look at previous research on pronominal anaphora. As mentioned above, this phenomenon has mainly been treated within the various frameworks of generative syntax, and it should therefore be appropriate to start with the earliest version of this, the so-called Standard Theory. Some analyses of anaphora in pragmatic frameworks have been attempted in recent years, but since these are few and relatively unimportant, an examination of these will be postponed until Chapter 4.

## 2.1 *The Standard Theory of Transformational Grammar*

### 2.1.1 *Definition of the Pronominalization Transformation*

The Standard Theory of transformational-generative grammar as outlined in Chomsky (1957, 1965) and elsewhere, is obviously influenced by the traditional school grammarian's view of a pronoun. This is reflected in the origin of this word from Latin *pronomen* via French *pronom*, i.e. 'for (instead of) a noun'. This view can also be found in the definition of this word, e.g. in the *Concise Oxford Dictionary* (1966):

> (7) pronoun: word used instead of (proper or other) noun to designate person or thing already mentioned or known from context or forming the subject of inquiry.[4]

That is, the Standard Theory claims that not only does a pronoun refer to a full noun which it is used instead of, it *is,* at some level of analysis, this very noun. Since this theory posits (at least) two levels of syntactic structure, deep and surface structure, it is possible to postulate a full NP in deep structure, which is then substituted by a pronoun in surface structure by a transformational operation. This transformation is called Pronominalization, and the approach under discussion is thus aptly called the Pronominalization Hypothesis.

Lees and Klima (1963) provided the first, and by now classic, article on pronominalization within this framework. They formulated the Pronominalization transformation as follows:

(8) X-Nom-Y-Nom'-Z →
X-Nom-Y-Nom' + Pron-Z

where Nom = Nom', and Nom is in a matrix sentence while Nom' is in a constituent sentence embedded in that matrix sentence (p. 23).

This transformation states that the second of two NPs that are coindexed in underlying structure will be turned into a pronoun. For example, an underlying structure like (9) will be turned into the surface structure in (10) by the Pronominalization transformation:

(9)   *Peter* thought that *Peter* was stupid.

(10) *Peter* thought that *he* was stupid.[5]

The reason why it is emphasized in (8) that the two NPs must belong to different clauses is the consideration in this article of the processes of Reflexivization and Reciprocals, which are also extensively dealt with by Lees and Klima. In the case where the two NPs are clause mates, Reflexivization will occur, changing the underlying structure represented in (11) into its surface form in (12).

(11)  *Peter* looked at *Peter*.

(12)  *Peter* looked at *himself.*

It is also important to note that implicit in this formulation of Pronominalization is the assumption that all semantic information is present at the underlying level. That means that all NPs are somehow associated with indices, e.g. $i$ and $j$, at deep structure, and that these indices cannot be changed by transformations. Syntactic processes, therefore, should not be able to alter the coreference options of two NPs; if they are coindexed at deep structure they should also be able to corefer at surface structure, and vice versa.

In this early version of transformational grammar, it was, however, also observed that some transformations could both create and destroy the environment for coreferential interpretation. This is the case in (13) and (14) below, where the transformations Extraposition and Passive[6] respectively have applied in the (b) versions, the former destroying and the latter creating the possibility of coreference between the pronoun and the full NP.

(13)  a.  That *Peter* won the game surprised *him*.
      b.*It surprised *him* that *Peter* won the game.

(14)  a.*\*She* kissed the man who *Leslie* was going to marry.
      b.  The man who *Leslie* was going to marry was kissed by *her*.

The explanation given for the data in (13) and (14) was based on rule ordering (see sections 2.3 and 2.4), but it is important even at this point to mention this quite disturbing fact. It seems contradictory and theoretically undesirable that the coreference possibilities of pronouns and full NPs are determined in derived structure, while all coreference information is present in the semantic component at deep structure. This paradox was going to create substantial problems for the Pronominalization Hypothesis and eventually lead to its rejection.

### 2.1.2   *Some Problems with the Standard Theory Approach*

Although the Standard Theory approach to pronominalization captures a very important generalization, namely that a pronoun usually refers to an entity which has been introduced by a full NP in the same sentence (unless, of course, it is a deictic pronoun,[7] about which Lees and Klima had nothing to say), it was soon discovered that the phenomenon is not quite as simple as indicated in the preceding section.

Firstly, Lees and Klima's Pronominalization rule only accounts for so-called forwards pronominalization,[8] i.e. the NP which triggers the process must occur in front of the NP which undergoes it, as in sentences (9) and (10) above. There are, however, also instances of backwards pronominalization,[8] as illustrated in the following examples:

(15)  That *he* was unpopular didn't bother *Peter*.

(16)  The man who kissed *her* liked *Leslie*.

Secondly, the matrix versus embedded clause condition on coreference does not hold either, as shown in the following two examples. In sentence (17) the two NPs belong to two conjoined sentences, whereas in sentence (18) the pronoun is actually in the matrix and the antecedent in the embedded clause.

(17)  *Peter* likes fish, but *he* also likes meat.

(18)  The man who kissed *Leslie* liked *her*.

It is also possible in certain cases for Pronominalization to occur instead of Reflexivization, when the NPs belong to the same clause, as in:

(19)  a.  *Mary's* brother likes *her*.
       b.*Mary's* brother likes *herself*.

The conclusion must therefore be that the Pronominalization transformation as stated in (8) undergenerates, in that there are several cases of pronominalization that it cannot account for.

## 2.2   *Langacker's Precede-and-Command Relations*

To remedy some of the weaknesses of the Pronominalization Hypothesis mentioned in the preceding section, Langacker (1969) abandons the matrix versus embedded clause condition and instead introduces some constraints on Pronominalization which he calls 'precede-and-command', also known as 'primacy relations'. The constraint is formulated as follows:

(20)  $NP^a$ may be used to pronominalize $NP^p$ unless $NP^p$ bears all relevant primacy relations to $NP^a$, i.e. $NP^p$ may not both precede and command $NP^a$.

-where $NP^a$ is the antecedent and $NP^p$ the pronoun (p. 173).

Langacker defines the command relation as (21):

(21)  A node A 'commands' another node B if
       (1)  neither A nor B dominates the other; and
       (2)  the S-node that most immediately dominates A also dominates B (p. 167).

Restriction (20) thus explains the coreference options of the NPs in the following four sentences, the structures of which are shown in the (b) versions:[9]

(22)  a. *Leslie* likes the man who kissed *her*.

b.

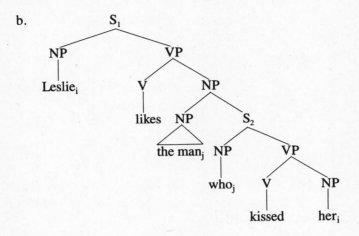

(23)  a. The man who kissed *Leslie* likes *her*.

b.

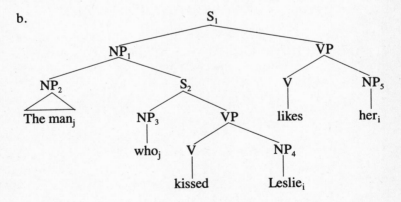

(24)  a. The man who kissed *her* likes *Leslie*.

b.

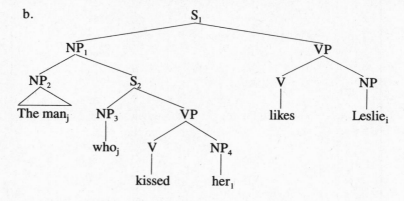

(25)  a. *She likes the man who kissed *Leslie*.

b.

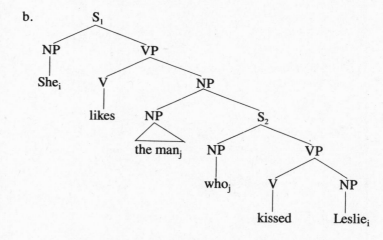

In (22), the pronoun *her* neither precedes nor commands the full NP *Leslie*, and the sentence is correctly predicted to be grammatical. In (23), the pronoun commands its antecedent, i.e. the S-node ($S_1$) most immediately dominating $NP_5$ also dominates $NP_4$, but since it does not also precede, this sentence is also grammatical. The opposite situation holds in (24); the pronoun precedes but does not command its antecedent, since $NP_4$ only commands the elements within the relative clause. In (25), however, both primacy relations are fulfilled in that the pronoun both precedes and commands its antecedent, and restriction (20) will correctly block the generation of this sentence.

## 2.3   *A Note on Pronominalization and Rule Ordering*

In the Standard Theory of transformational-generative grammar, rules are assumed to apply in an unordered fashion whenever their structural description is met, subject only to the restriction of the cycle, i.e. all transformations apply first to the most deeply embedded S, then to the next (adjacent) S up the tree and so on until the topmost S has been reached. The Principle of Strict Cyclicity ensures that no transformation may apply on a given cycle wholly within the domain of another cycle. Although most transformations are of the cyclical type, some rules are found to be precyclical (although precyclical rules have been a quite controversial issue in the standard framework), i.e. applying before all cyclical rules, whereas other rules must be postcyclical, i.e. applying to the whole tree simultaneously after all cyclical rules have applied. The cycle-type of Pronominalization was also of great concern to generative grammarians in the 1960s. The data presented in this section, discovered by Ross (1969), led linguists to the conclusion that Pronominalization had to be a cyclical rule.

Ross (1967) formulated a constraint on Pronominalization in terms of the notion 'subordinate clause', which produces basically the same results as Langacker's precede-and-command condition. Ross's constraint was formulated as (26):

> (26)  If one element precedes another, the second can only pronominalize the first if the first is dominated by a subordinate clause which does not dominate the second (p. 358).

He thus claims that forwards pronominalization is free, whereas backwards pronominalization is sometimes blocked (by the condition stated in (26)). This is illustrated in the sentences below, the (a) version being the underlying structure, and the (b) and (c) versions the results after forwards and backwards pronominalization respectively.

> (27)  a.  That *Peter* was unpopular didn't disturb *Peter*.
>        b.  That *Peter* was unpopular didn't disturb *him*.
>        c.  That *he* was unpopular didn't disturb *Peter*.

> (28)  a.  *Peter* was hungry after *Peter* woke up.
>        b.  *Peter* was hungry after *he* woke up.
>        c.\**He* was hungry after *Peter* woke up.

None of the sentences in (27) violate the subordinate clause condition and are therefore all grammatical. In (28), however, the two NPs stand in a relationship not compatible with the constraint, i.e. the first NP is not dominated by a 'subordinate clause'. Backwards pronominalization is thus blocked, and a sentence like (28c) cannot be generated.

There are, unfortunately, cases where also forwards pronominalization seems to be blocked. Consider for example the following sentences and compare them with those in (27):

> (29) a. Realizing that *Peter* was unpopular didn't disturb *Peter*.
> b.*Realizing that *Peter* was unpopular didn't disturb *him*.
> c. Realizing that *he* was unpopular didn't disturb *Peter*.

To explain (29), in which Pronominalization interacts with the transformation EQUI (NP Deletion), one must posit the following underlying structure:

(30)

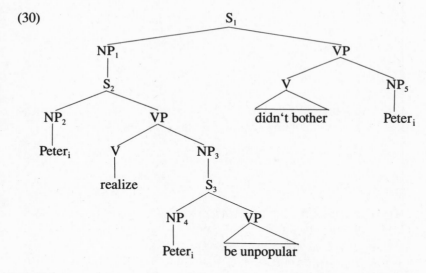

Working cyclically up the tree, we find that the structural description for Pronominalization is first met on the cycle of $S_1$ where it obligatorily applies, pronominalizing the NP in $S_3$. On the cycle of $S_1$, the structural description is met for EQUI, which deletes $NP_2$ in the lower clause under identity with $NP_5$. The result of these processes is the sentence represented in (29c). The ungrammatical (29b) would have to be derived by applying EQUI first and then Pronominalization on the cycle of $S_1$, treating Pronominalization in this case as a postcyclical rule in order not to violate the Principle of Strict Cyclicity. As this is obviously the wrong approach, we see that to avoid the derivation of such sentences as (29b), Pronominalization must be considered a cyclical rule.

It must be noted, however, that surface structures like (29b), i.e. without coreference between the pronoun and the full NP, may of course be generated. The corresponding underlying structure must in those cases look like the following, assuming that pronouns that are not derived by the Pronominalization transformation are produced by the phrase structure rules and are thus present already at deep structure:

(31)

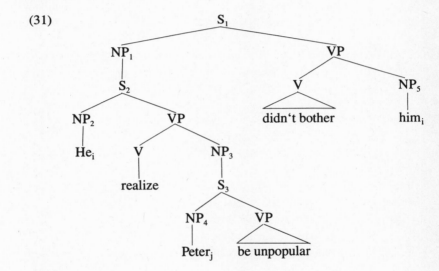

## 2.4  Problems with the Pronominalization Hypothesis

There are three major problems with the Pronominalization Hypothesis which all contributed to the fall of this particular transformation within the framework of the Extended Standard Theory (EST), which was the development of the transformational-generative model in the 1970s. The first difficulty with this hypothesis arises exactly in connection with the aspect of rule ordering discussed in the preceding section.

As shown above, Ross gives quite convincing evidence that Pronominalization must be a cyclical rule. Unfortunately for this analysis, there are contradictory data on this point. Sentences like those in (13) in section 2.1.1, repeated below for convenience, indicate that Pronominalization must be a postcyclical rule:

(32)  a.  That *Peter* won the game surprised *him*.
     b.*It surprised *him* that *Peter* won the game.

That is, Pronominalization must be prevented from applying before Extraposition in (32), since the latter transformation is incompatible with the conditions on the former. As both transformations in (32) apply on the same cycle (the topmost S), the non-derivation of (32b) can only be achieved by considering Pronominalization as a postcyclical rule.

Other data provide us with evidence that Pronominalization must be a *pre*-cyclical rule. This is the only solution—in the present framework—if we want to avoid the derivation of the ungrammatical (d) version from the underlying (a) version of (33), where Pronominalization interacts with *there*-Insertion:

(33)  a.  *A woman* believes that *a woman* will be elected.
     b.  *A woman* believes that *she* will be elected.
     c.  *A woman* believes that there will be *a woman* elected.[10]
     d.*A woman* believes that there will be *she* elected.

In this case, *there*-Insertion must apply on the cycle of $S_2$, while the structural description for Pronominalization is not met until one reaches the cycle of $S_1$. Only if Pronominalization is allowed to apply precyclically can the application of *there*-Insertion, which usually only applies with indefinite NPs, be blocked and the ungrammatical sentence never generated.

The above data, indicating that Pronominalization can be considered both pre- and postcyclical as well as a cyclical rule, weakened the Pronominalization Hypothesis considerably, as it was of course impossible to maintain all three versions of the cycle-type of this transformation simultaneously. Accepting only one, on the other hand, would lead to undesirable outputs.

While the first of the objections to the Pronominalization Hypothesis was grounded on empirical data, the other two difficulties connected with this approach are based on theory-internal problems. The first one concerns the nature of the device that would have to mark elements as coreferential or non-coreferential in underlying structure. There would have to be a mechanism giving identical or distinct indices to two nominal elements, regardless of whether they are pronouns or full NPs, as for example in the following two sentences:

(34) He thinks he is stupid.

(35) Peter thinks Peter is stupid.

The two NPs in both (34) and (35) may either refer to the same individual, in which case they would be coindexed, or to two different individuals, in which case they would receive distinct indices in underlying structure.

It is reasonable to assume that this mechanism would apply not only between two pronouns or two full NPs, but also between a pronoun and a full NP in the same sentence, unless some special construction was introduced to prevent it. Such a construction would, however, be a completely *ad hoc* device with no independent motivation. Seen in this perspective, the Pronominalization transformation would actually be superfluous, as all sentences with full NPs and pronouns, both the grammatical ones and the ones we would wish to block with the precede-and-command condition, would be derivable directly from underlying structures.

The final shortcoming of this hypothesis that I would like to mention here is the mere fact that there are important aspects of anaphora that are left unexplained by it. It is for example highly implausible semantically that sentence (36) is derived from (37), yet this is what the Pronominalization Hypothesis would have to postulate.

(36) Most people think that they are intelligent.

(37) Most people think that most people are intelligent.

## 2.5  *From Transformation to Semantic Interpretive Rule*

Starting with Chomsky's 'Conditions on Transformations' (1973) and later 'Conditions on Rules of Grammar'(1976), the whole framework of generative grammar changed direction in the 1970s. Now transformations were supposed to apply blindly, restricted only by very general constraints like the Tensed S Condition, the Specified Subject Condition and Subjacency. Also at this time, the introduction into this grammatical model of the component of Logical Form, a semantic component present at surface structure, resulted in the reanalysis of certain transformations as semantic interpretive rules. These included Reflexivization, the Reciprocal rule, EQUI and Pronominalization, since these were all rules that could not apply blindly, but needed to make reference to coreferential elements and coindexing.

This new approach to Pronominalization, or the *anaphora rule* as it was increasingly called to avoid the connotation of a transformational process, assumes that all pronouns, deictic as well as anaphoric, are present in deep structure. No NPs bear an index at this level, however, but the anaphora rule, which now works in the semantic component, interprets two NPs as coreferential or non-coreferential, subject to the precede-and-command condition, and assigns indices accordingly.

When pronouns are assumed to be already present at deep structure, the previously mentioned problems of rule ordering and cyclicity are no longer an issue for the phenomenon of anaphoric relations.[11] Sentences like Ross's (29c) and (29b), repeated below for convenience, will now simply be subject to the anaphora rule in Logical Form, which will interpret the the two NPs as coreferential in the surface form of the former sentence and as non-coreferential in the latter.

(38)  Realizing that *he* was unpopular didn't bother *Peter*.

(39)*Realizing that *Peter* was unpopular didn't bother *him*.

A sentence like (33d), repeated below as (40), may also be more easily explained now. The ungrammaticality of the sentence is in fact not due to Pronominalization at all, but rather to the fact that *there*-Insertion has been applied inappropriately. This transformation may, in most cases at least, only occur with indefinite NPs (cf. above), and indefiniteness is not a property that is normally ascribed to pronouns.

(40)**A woman* believes that there will be *she* elected.

In this EST approach to anaphora, there was consensus among linguists as to where the rule was to apply, i.e. to the surface structure trees after all transformations had been applied. There was more discussion about the actual formulation of the rule(s), however. Jackendoff (1972) made an important contribution in this respect. He posited two rules, an optional rule of Coreference Assignment, which was subject to the precede-and-command condition, and an obligatory rule of Distinct Reference Assignment. The latter rule simply applied to all NPs that had not been marked by the previous rule.

Lasnik (1976) adopted a slightly different approach. He claimed that only a rule of Distinct Reference Assignment was needed to explain the non-anaphoric relationship between the pronoun and the full NP in a sentence like the following:

(41) He bought a car before Peter left town.

The pronominal reference in (42), however, is comparable to that in (43), in that the semantics of the sentence simply does not specify who the pronoun refers to, but rather allows it to be used to refer to any individual (including the one referred to by the full NP) whose identity can be inferred from the situation in which the sentence is uttered.

(42) Peter bought a car before he left town.

(43) He bought a car.

## 2.6   C-command: A New Restriction on Anaphora

### 2.6.1   Problems Connected with the Precede-and-Command Condition

Up to this point, linguists could differ considerably in their theoretical approach to the problem of pronominal reference, but there was still general agreement on the conditions governing anaphoric relations, namely Langacker's precede-and-command. In 1976, however, Tanya Reinhart, in her dissertation *The Syntactic Domain of Anaphora*, pointed out several problems with the old constraints on coreference and introduced a new and more explanatory condition on anaphora, which she called *c-command* (for constituent-command).

Reinhart first observed that the claim made by many linguists that only backwards pronominalization was restricted, whereas forwards pronominalization was free, is not correct, and she provided examples like the following to prove her point:

(44) Near *him*, *Peter* saw a snake.

(45) In *her* office, *Leslie* works night and day.

The above sentences are fully grammatical, although in (44) as well as in (45), the pronoun both precedes and commands its antecedent and the precede-and-command restriction would predict them both to be ungrammatical. If the full NP and the pronoun are interchanged, however, as in (46) and (47) below, the sentences become totally ungrammatical. As the pronoun no longer precedes and commands the full NP, this notion cannot account for the ungrammaticality of these sentences either.

(46)*Near *Peter*, *he* saw a snake.

(47)*In *Leslie's* office, *she* works night and day.

### 2.6.2   *C-command*

Reinhart explains the above sentences and similar examples by introducing the notion of c-command, the definition of which is the following:

(48) Node A c(onstituent)-commands node B iff the branching node most immediately dominating A also dominates B (Reinhart 1981, p. 612).

The difference between command and c-command lies basically in the fact that the latter chooses branching node whereas the former uses S-node as limits of control, and this can be illustrated in the following tree structure:

(49)

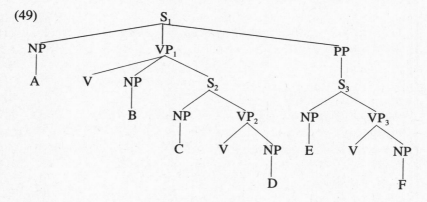

Nodes A and B both command the whole tree, whereas nodes C and D only command the elements in $S_2$, and E and F only the elements in $S_3$. In terms of c-command, only node A dominates the whole tree, whereas node B c-commands only the elements under $VP_1$. The c-command domains of the other nodes, C, D, E, and F, are thus $S_2$, $VP_2$, $S_3$ and $VP_3$ respectively.

Using English sentences as her data, Reinhart argues convincingly that, except in a few cases, the notion of c-command is the correct restriction on coreference between NPs. She formulates the constraint as follows:

(50) A given NP cannot be interpreted as coreferential with a distinct non-pronoun in its c-command domain (Reinhart 1981, p. 617).

It should be noted here that the notion of c-command is also used to explain the restrictions on so-called *bound anaphora*, i.e. the syntactic relationship between pronouns on the one hand and quantified NPs and *wh*-phrases on the other (see examples (5) and (6) above), as well as the Reflexive and Reciprocal processes (see examples (3) and (4)). The restrictions can be formulated as (51) and (52), and I leave it to the reader to go back and check that they can account for the grammaticality versus ungrammaticality of the sentences just referred to.

(51) Quantified NPs and *wh*-traces can have anaphoric relations only with pronouns in their c-command domain (i.e. a pronoun must be interpreted as coreferential with (and only with) a c-commanding NP, if that NP is a quantified NP or *wh*-trace, MRW) (Reinhart 1983b, p. 122).

(52) A reflexive or reciprocal pronoun (an R-pronoun) must be interpreted as coreferential with (and only with) a c-commanding NP within a specified syntactic domain (e.g. its minimal governing category) (Reinhart (1983b, p. 136).

### 2.6.3    *Differences Between Precede-and-Command and C-command*

One important difference between the precede-and-command and c-command restrictions on coreference is that the former makes reference to linear order, whereas the latter attempts to explain all coreference options strictly in terms of tree structure.[12] But since English is a right-branching language, the c-commanding node will very often precede the c-commanded node, and the two restrictions will thus make the same predictions for the majority of English sentences. There are only two cases where the two restrictions will differ:

(53) A. Sentences where the pronoun precedes and commands its antecedent, but does not c-command it.

B. Sentences where the pronoun c-commands, but does not precede its antecedent.

Examples of type A have already been given in (44) and (45), while examples (46) and (47) illustrate type B sentences. Together these sentences constitute a strong argument in favor of c-command, since this restriction correctly predicts type A sentences to be grammatical, while it rules out coreferential readings in type B sentences. It should be noted here that all these examples involve preposed PPs, which consequently play a crucial role in Reinhart's argumentation. Not all such elements behave as straightforwardly as indicated here, however, and they therefore deserve further attention. An extensive treatment of the structure of preposed PPs is given in Reinhart (1981), and this topic will also be discussed more thoroughly in Chapters 3 and 4.


## 2.7  *Anaphora Within the Theory of Government and Binding*

The most recent version of generative syntax is known as Government and Binding (or simply GB), and is also mainly due to the work of Chomsky (1980, 1981). Government and Binding is a modular theory, i.e. it consists of various principles and subsystems of principles that are assumed to be universal in character, e.g *theta*-theory, binding theory, Case[13] theory etc., as well as certain parameters that are supposed to account for variations among languages. The notion of c-command has a central role within this framework; it is for example the major part of the definition of *government*, and it has been found to be the relevant structural relationship between elements undergoing various syntactic processes (e.g. the NP and its trace in the only remaining transformation, 'Move $\alpha$').

The restriction on coreference between pronouns and full NPs is dealt with within the *binding* theory. Chomsky distinguishes between *anaphors* on the one hand, which include reciprocals and reflexives (as well as NP traces, which do not concern us here), and *pronominals* on the other. All NPs bear an index already at deep structure, which is merely randomly assigned.[14] In the component of Logical Form, NPs which are accidentally coindexed are interpreted according to the following restrictions:

(54) An anaphor is bound [ i.e. coindexed and c-commanded, MRW ] in its governing category.

(55) A pronominal is free in its governing category.

(56) An R-expression [full NP, MRW] is free.
(Chomsky 1981, p. 188).

The results required by (54)–(56), which basically produce the same outputs as Reinhart's c-command condition, are in this framework achieved not by coindexing procedures, but by general output conditions on appropriate coindexing (or binding). This means that in the case where a pronoun and a full NP happen to be coindexed but cannot be interpreted as coreferential according to the above conditions, the sentence will be 'thrown out' and never be able to reach the surface.

According to this approach, then, all pronouns in the following sentences must be defined as *free*:

(57) The man who kissed Leslie liked her.

(58) Leslie likes her.

(59) She likes the man who kissed Leslie.

But the original intention of the anaphora question was to distinguish (57) from the other two. In the present framework this has been left to the output conditions on binding, which will filter out (58) and (59) in the cases where the pronoun and full NP are accidentally coindexed.

In the cases where the pronoun may indeed corefer with the full NP, as in (57), the actual reference will be assigned by pragmatic factors, which, according to Chomsky, are outside the scope of grammar.[15]

# 3
# Problems with a Purely Syntactic Approach to Anaphora

## 3.0  *Introduction*

In the preceding chapter, I sketched the approximately twenty year old history of Pronominalization, or rather the intrasentential relationship between pronouns and full NPs, as this phenomenon has been looked upon within the framework of generative grammar. As indicated in the Introduction, however, I think there is more to be said about definite NP anaphora than is possible within this purely syntactic approach. In the present chapter, therefore, I shall discuss the various theory-internal and empirical problems connected with this approach, some of which have been recognized by these linguists themselves.

## 3.1  *Empirical Problems*

Although Reinhart's c-command restriction on coreference between pronouns and full NPs quite elegantly captures many of the often intricate reference options of NPs in sentences, there are also quite a few empirical problems connected with it. By this I mean that there are data that are left unexplained by the theory or that the condition actually produces undesirable outputs.

### 3.1.1  *Preposed PPs*

The overwhelming majority of sentences that Reinhart (1976 and elsewhere) invokes to argue against the precede-and-command condition of Langacker and in favor of her own restriction on anaphora defined in terms of c-command, are sentences with preposed PPs. In (60), for example, where a pronoun precedes and commands, but does not c-command the full NP, the sentence is nevertheless grammatical with coreference.

(60) In *his* kitchen, *Peter* cooks the most wonderful dishes.

If the full NP and the pronoun switch places, the pronoun is in a position where it c-commands, but no longer precedes the full NP, and the resulting sentence is, again according to Reinhart's prediction, ungrammatical:

(61) *In *Peter's* kitchen, *he* cooks the most wonderful dishes.

But as indicated above, not all sentences with preposed PPs behave as straight-forwardly as this. Reinhart noted that seemingly identical PPs behave differently with respect to their coreference options, as illustrated by the following sentences:

(62)  In *Peter's* home town, *he* is still considered a good actor.

(63)  *In *Peter's home town, he* spent most of his life.

Reinhart explains this disparity in grammaticality by positing a structural difference between sentential PPs, which in the tree structure are attached to the S-node, and verb phrasal PPs, which as the name suggests, are attached to the VP. This difference in grammaticality can also be noted before the PPs have been preposed. Consider for example the following sentences and their respective tree structures:

(64) a.  They still consider *him* a good actor in *Peter's* home town.

b.
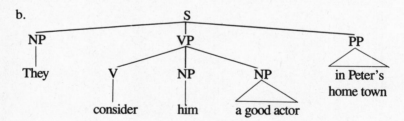

(65) a.*They let *him* spend most of his life in *Peter's* home town.

b.
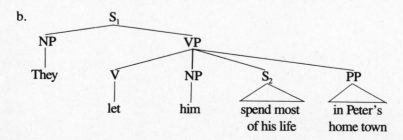

The difference in grammaticality between (64) and (65) can be accounted for by this structural difference between sentential and verb phrasal PPs: the PP in (65) is attached to the VP and is thus within the c-command domain of the pronoun in object position, and coreference is therefore blocked. In (64), on the other hand, the PP is attached to the S-node and thus falls outside the scope of the pronoun.

Reinhart then claims that unlike all other movement analyses in the present framework, this structural difference is also maintained when the PPs are pre-posed. Verb phrasal PPs are, as would be expected of all preposed elements, moved into COMP position, whereas a sentential PP is attached to some higher projection of S ($\bar{\bar{S}}$). To account for the coreference options of these PPs, then, Reinhart needs to extend the original definition of c-command, an extension which is not independently motivated by any other linguistic facts and not adopted for any other aspects of the theory of Government and Binding either. [16] The extended definition of c-command is formulated as follows:

(66) Node A c(onstituent)-commands node B iff the branching node $\alpha_1$ most immediately dominating A either dominates B or is immediately dominated by a node $\alpha_2$ which dominates B, and $\alpha_2$ is of the same category type as $\alpha_1$ (Reinhart 1981, p. 612).

We may now go back to our problematic sentences (62) and (63), which, according to Reinhart's analysis, have the following surface structures:

(67)

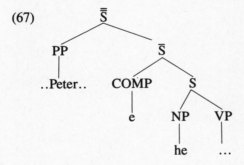

(68)

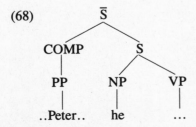

Coreference is possible in (62) (corresponding to the structure in (67)), since the sentential PP is outside the c-command domain of the subject pronoun (c-command can only be extended to the next branching node up of the same category type, i.e. to $\bar{S}$ in this case). Sentence (63), on the other hand, is ungrammatical with coreference, since, according to Reinhart's extended definition, the subject has scope over material in the COMP position, in this case the verb phrasal PP.

It does not seem easy to find evidence for this structural difference between sentential and verb phrasal PPs. Reinhart supports her postulation by referring to various syntactic tests such as *though*-Movement, *wh*-Movement and VP Preposing,[17] the most successful, however, being Pseudo-clefting. This type of construction involves extrapositioning of material in the verb phrase only, while the initial *wh*-clause may not contain anything from this constituent. Sentence (69a) is thus ungrammatical because a sentential PP has been clefted together with the VP, while (70b) is ungrammatical (in the intended reading)[18] because the verb phrasal PP has not been clefted together with the rest of the VP, but is still part of the *wh*-clause.

(69) a.*What Leslie did was ride a horse in Peter's picture.
     b. What Leslie did was find a scratch in Peter's picture.

(70) a. What Leslie did in Peter's picture was ride a horse.
     b.*What Leslie did in Peter's picture was find a scratch.

I would like to claim, however, that there are several indeterminate cases in this respect, and that the difference between sentential and verb phrasal PPs is not quite as clear-cut as pure syntacticians would have us believe. Consider for example the following sentences, which are all grammatical in spite of the fact that the PP in question has been clefted together with the VP in the (b) versions of (71) and (72), while it belongs to the *wh*-clause in the (a) versions:

(71) a. What Peter did in his kitchen was cook many wonderful dishes.
     b. What Peter did was cook many wonderful dishes in his kitchen.

(72) a. What Peter is in his home town is a highly respected person.
     b. What Peter is is a highly respected person in his home town.

### 3.1.2 *Subject/Non-subject Asymmetry*

The most elegant aspect of Reinhart's notion of c-command concerning anaphora is perhaps that it accounts for the subject/non-subject asymmetry which puzzled generative linguists for a long time. This asymmetry, which is illustrated in sentences (73) and (74), is predictable under Reinhart's approach, since the syntactic domain of the subject is the whole sentence, whereas the domain of, say, the object is only the VP.

(73) a. They caught *him* before *Peter* had a chance to get away.
b.\**He* was caught before *Peter* had a chance to get away.

(74) a. They consider *him* a good actor in *Peter's* home town.
b.\**He* is considered a good actor in *Peter's* home town.

Sentences (73a) and (74a) are thus correctly predicted to be grammatical since the (sentential) adverbials in both sentences are outside the c-command domain of the object, but coreference must be blocked in (73b) and (74b) since the subject c-commands everything under S.

But although c-command is an extremely elegant condition, its most serious shortcoming, in my opinion, is precisely this subject/non-subject asymmetry. McCawley (1984) points out that while Reinhart's suggested structural difference between preposed sentential and verb phrasal PPs nicely accounts for the difference in coreference options when the pronoun is in subject position, the notion of c-command does not explain why this difference remains when the pronoun is in object position. Compare for example the following sentences with (62) and (63) above:

(75) In *Peter's* home town, they still consider *him* a good actor.

(76) \*In *Peter's* home town, they let *him* spend most of his life.

In (75) and (76), no c-command is involved, and the anaphora rule would not block the derivation of either. McCawley's solution to this is a discontinuous structure for sentence (76) like the one represented in (77), which in my opinion is one that allows too much. Unless one accepts this, however, there is no way the c-command condition on anaphora can be used to explain these, for Reinhart's theory, rather dismaying facts.

(77)

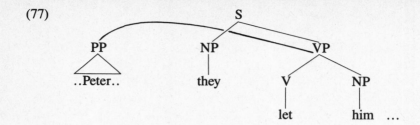

### 3.1.3   *Other PP Problems*

Another problem concerning PPs is discussed by Reinhart herself and illustrated by the following examples:

(78) a.*It didn't bother *her* that *Leslie* failed the exam.

b.

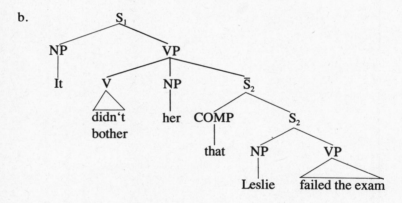

(79) a.*It didn't occur to *her* that *Leslie* failed the exam.

b.

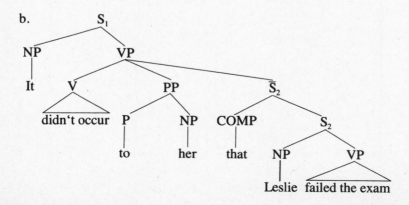

Coreference is equally impossible in both of the above sentences although the pronoun in (79) is dominated by a PP and thus does not c-command the full NP in the embedded clause. Reinhart tries to explain this by postulating a structural difference between regular PPs and PPs like the above, which function as indirect objects. The latter are claimed to be dominated by an NP in underlying structure, as in many other languages, and simply happen to be lexically realized with a preposition in English. This, I find, is a fairly reasonable suggestion, but unfortunately it fails to account for the fact that both (80) and (81) are ungrammatical, since only in (80) can the PP containing the pronoun be interpreted as an indirect object.

(80) *I talked to *him* about *John*.

(81) *I talked about *him* to *John*.

Also in the following two examples, the pronouns are embedded under a PP and thus do not c-command their antecedents, and coreference should be possible. Reinhart's NP-account of indirect object PPs does not hold here either, since the PPs in these cases are clearly locative.

(82) *I went to *him* to talk about *Peter's* problems.

(83) *I walked over to *her* in *Leslie's* garden.

Another shortcoming of Reinhart's solution is that it contradicts itself. If all PPs that can be interpreted as indirect objects are dominated by an NP in underlying structure—to account for sentences like (79) and (80)—the structure of the PP in (84) should be identical to the PPs in those sentences, and the pronoun should be able to c-command its antecedent. In this case, however, we need the preposition to block c-command and allow coreference, since the sentence is obviously grammatical.

(84) I gave *John's* dog back to *him*.

### 3.1.4  *Subjacency*

A problem mentioned by both Reinhart and McCawley concerns the question of whether the anaphora rule obeys subjacency, a principle in the most recent version of generative grammar which supposedly subsumes all the previous island constraints discovered by Ross (1967) (except the Coordinate Structure Constraint). Subjacency is a condition on rules that can be stated as (85), and which was originally meant only to constrain movement rules:[19]

(85) *Subjacency*

No rule may involve X and Y in the structure

$$...X...[_\alpha...[_\beta...Y..._\beta]..._\alpha]...$$

where $\alpha$ and $\beta$ are cyclic nodes (NP and S).

Sentences like the following do in fact indicate that the anaphora rule, although it is an interpretive rule applying in Logical Form, does obey subjacency:

(86) *Near *Peter, *he* found a snake.

(87) Near $[_{NP}$ the garage that $[_S$ *Peter* had built $_S]_{NP}]$, *he* found a snake.

But when one takes a closer look at sentences like the above, one discovers that there is a subject/non-subject asymmetry here as well, which Reinhart's subjacency solution cannot account for:

(88) They found *him* in $[_{NP}$ the garage that $[_S$ *Peter* had built $_S]_{NP}]$.

(89) *He* was found in $[_{NP}$ the garage that $[_S$ *Peter* had built $_S]_{NP}]$.

Both in (88) and (89) the pronoun c-commands the full NP in the embedded clause, but since this NP is subjacent to the pronoun, coreference should be possible if we assume that the anaphora rule is sensitive to subjacency. However, coreference is not possible in (89), where the pronoun is in subject position, and this suggests that there is more to be said about the subject/non-subject asymmetry than is possible in terms of c-command.

## 3.2  *Theory-internal Problems*

So far I have sketched some problems with Reinhart's purely syntactic analysis of anaphora which are mainly of an empirical nature. These suggest that the notion of c-command is not perfect and that it should somehow be modified or redefined to accommodate these linguistic problems. In this section I would like to discuss a different, and in my opinion more serious, type of problem connected with this analysis. This concerns theory-internal problems, which indicate, I would like to claim, that a purely syntactic approach to anaphora not only runs into data problems, but rather that its rests on false premises.

### 3.2.1   *Grammaticality Judgements*

#### 3.2.1.1   *General Problems*

One of the most fundamental problems with a purely syntactic approach to anaphora, in my opinion, is that it completely disregards the great vacillation in grammaticality judgements concerning these sentences. Only a small number of the sentences with definite NP anaphora cited in the literature are clear-cut examples that everybody either totally rejects or accepts; for the majority of these sentences there is great disagreement among speakers.[20] My hypothesis, therefore, is that people do not accept and reject sentences on the basis of some internalized syntactic structure, but that their grammaticality judgements depend on whether or not they can construct a context in which the sentence in question would be pragmatically plausible. This especially concerns sentences with preposed PPs, which are crucial for the notion of c-command, but unfortunately for Reinhart's analysis, they are fairly indeterminate as to their grammaticality. Consider for example the following sentences:

(90) In the big picture of *Leslie, she* found several scratches.

(91) With *Leslie's* new peacock feather, *she* was tickling Peter all night.

Both (90) and (91) are supposed to be ungrammatical according to Reinhart's analysis, since both PPs must necessarily be verb phrasal[21] and therefore in the c-command domain of the subject when preposed. Several native speakers that I have consulted, however, claim that while the above sentences are not exactly wonderful, they are not 'absolutely terrible' either.[22]

A theory of language like that of Langacker (1984), which is built on an analysis of human cognition, would appear to account for the above facts. In this analysis, linguistic constructions are viewed as having more or less *unit* status, and it is thus predicted that there will be a hierarchy of acceptability in languages according to the status of the construction in question. In this respect, therefore, I accept Langacker's theory.

### 3.2.1.2 *Possessive NPs*

Much of the disagreement on grammaticality concerns sentences with possessive NPs like the following:

(92) a. *His* mother likes *Peter*.

b.

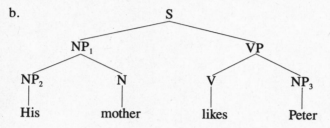

Some people accept (92) as grammatical, which is as expected if one adopts Reinhart's original definition of c-command, i.e. the domain of $NP_2$ does not extend any further up the tree than $NP_1$, and the pronoun thus does not c-command its antecedent. However, other people totally reject sentences like (92).

Although the grammaticality judgements for (92) are fairly unequivocal, there is much more vacillation and a stronger tendency to accept sentences like (93a) and (94a). The structures of these sentences, represented in (93b) and (94b), reveal that the syntactic relationship between the pronoun and the full NP is nevertheless identical to that of (92), and this again suggests that grammaticality cannot be determined solely on the basis of syntax.

(93) a. *His* mother thinks that *Peter* is a genius.

b.

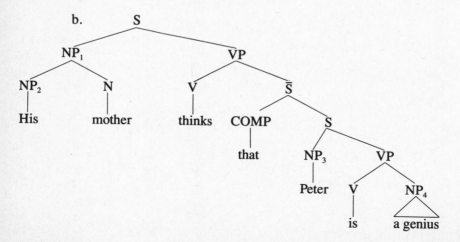

(94) a. We used *her* scissors to cut *Leslie's* hair.

b.

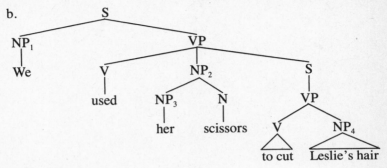

### 3.2.1.3   *Consistency*

One could claim that the disagreement concerning the grammaticality of sentences with possessive NPs lies in a difference between various speakers' internalized definition of c-command; some accept only the original definition in which the domain of a certain node cannot be extended to a node of the same category type higher up in the tree, whereas others have internalized a modified, and thus more restrictive, definition of c-command which allows the determiner of a possessive NP to have the same syntactic domain as the higher NP. If this were true, one would expect it to be consistent in other cases as well.

This can be tested by considering a related problem, namely the coreference options of pronouns and quantified NPs. As mentioned above (see section 2.6.2), this phenomenon is in the Government and Binding framework treated as bound anaphora, and the restriction on coreference (stated as (51) above) briefly says that for the pronoun and quantified NP to corefer, the latter must c-command the former. This is illustrated in the following sentence:

(95) a. *Everyone* thinks *he* is a genius.

b.

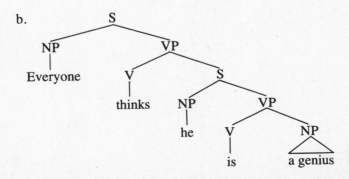

When the quantified NP is possessive, as in (96), the grammaticality of the sentence should depend on the definition of c-command; i.e. people who reject (92) should accept (96) and vice versa.

(96) a. *Everyone's* mother likes *him*.

b.
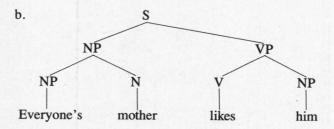

This prediction, however, turns out to be false. During a class lecture[23] with approximately twenty-five native speakers of English present, it was observed that there was no necessary correlation between the grammaticality judgements and definitions of c-command, i.e. those who accepted one of the sentences did not necessarily reject the other. Most of the students actually accepted both (92) and (96), and this creates quite a dilemma for Reinhart's analysis. To account for (92), then, we need the original definition of c-command, while an *ad hoc* modification of this definition is needed to account for (96).

### 3.2.1.4  *Preposed Adverbials Revisited*

The final problem of grammaticality related to Reinhart's solution for preposed PPs (see 3.1.1 above) that I would like to mention here, concerns the cases where a sentential adverbial (PP or other) is embedded under a verb phrasal one. Reinhart's prediction is that when such a sentential adverbial is preposed, it should behave like a verb phrasal one (since it, under a movement analysis, originates under the VP), and should thus be within the c-command domain of the subject. She is therefore forced to claim that sentence (97) is ungrammatical, while (98) is acceptable:

(97) *When *Leslie* finishes school, *she* has promised Peter to go to New York.

(98)  When *she* finishes school, *Leslie* has promised Peter to go to New York.

Reinhart admits that there is considerable vacillation in the grammaticality judgements here, and that many speakers of American English do not accept either of the above sentences. Personally, I find both (97) and (98) equally acceptable, and I have found several native speakers who agree with me. A further example of the uncertainty here is that one British speaker that I asked about this claimed that (97) was 'definitely [his] idea of a perfect sentence.'

### 3.2.2  Ordering[24]

The question of the anaphora rule and its ordering in relation to other transformations posed a problem to generative linguists for a long time. In the early versions of transformational grammar, this was formulated as the question of the cycle-type of Pronominalization, but after the Pronominalization Hypothesis was abandoned, and pronouns were assumed to be present in deep structure, this problem seemed to disappear. Reinhart's anaphora rule is a semantic interpretive rule applying in the semantic component called Logical Form. According to the most recent model of generative grammar, which can schematically be represented as (99), this rule must apply to surface structures (S-structures) after all syntactic transformations have applied.

(99)

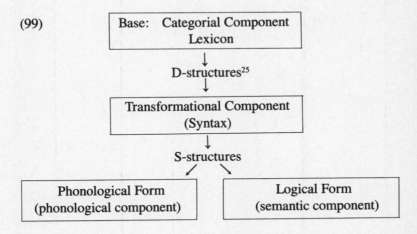

As I indicated in Chapter 2, however, this approach is not able to solve all ordering problems concerning anaphora. The following two sentences, for example, are ungrammatical with coreference, although there are no relevant c-command relations involved in their respective surface structures. Reinhart's rule would therefore incorrectly predict both of them to be grammatical.

(100) a.*What *she* believes is that *Leslie* is irresistible.

b.

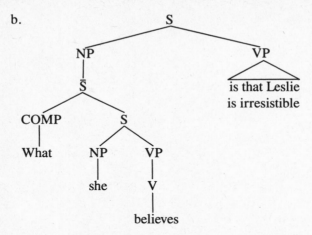

(101) a.*In *Peter's* apartment, we think *he* smokes pot.[26]

b.

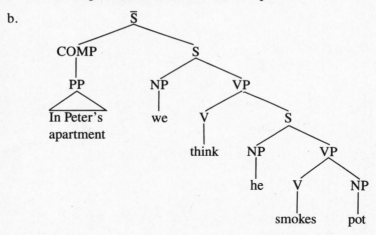

As long as the anaphora rule is only allowed to apply to surface structures, there is no way sentences (100) and (101) can be accounted for in the present analysis. One solution which immediately comes to mind, is to allow the rule to apply directly to deep structures, i.e. before the Pseudo-cleft and PP Preposing transformations respectively. When one considers the c-command relations of (100) and (101) at deep structure, represented in (102) and (103) below, it becomes clear that this solution would work for these sentences and ensure that they would never be able to reach the surface, but be thrown out already at some underlying level.

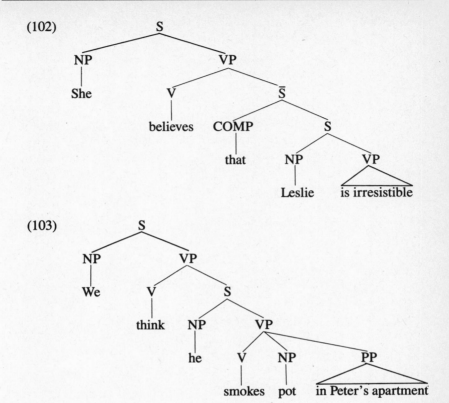

(102)

(103)

It is not difficult, however, to find counterarguments to this solution. Many sentences are grammatical at deep structure, but turned into ungrammatical ones by the application of various transformations. This solution would therefore not be able to account for the ungrammaticality of (105) and (107), which are derived by Extraposition and Passive respectively from the fully grammatical sources (104) and (106).

(104)   That *Leslie* was elected surprised *her*.

(105)   *It surprised *her* that *Leslie* was elected.

(106)   The people that elected *Leslie* surprised *her*.

(107)   *She* was surprised by the people that elected *Leslie*.

What the data in (104)-(107) suggest, then, is that the anaphora rule should be allowed to apply at every stage in the derivation, i.e. after each transformation in the syntactic component (or, to be more specific, after each application of 'Move $\alpha$', which is the only remaining transformation in the present version of the framework).[27] Some kind of mechanism would thus be needed in the syntactic component to throw out sentences once they turn ungrammatical. Unfortunately for Reinhart's analysis, this solution does not work either, since in addition to the duplication problem (it should be unnecessary for the same rules and principles to apply more than once in the derivation of a sentence), this solution could not account for sentences that are ungrammatical at some point in the derivation, but rendered grammatical by the application of a transformation. This situation is illustrated in (108), where the ungrammatical source is converted into a grammatical sentence by the transformation PP Preposing.

(108) a.*_She_ is wearing a blue dress in _Leslie's_ wedding picture.
      b. In _Leslie's_ wedding picture, _she_ is wearing a blue dress.

In the light of the above examples, therefore, we are forced to conclude that Reinhart's analysis of anaphora in the Government and Binding framework has not really been able to solve this old ordering problem. This weakness provides yet another argument against a purely syntactic approach to this phenomenon.

### 3.2.3  _Coordinate Structures_

Both Reinhart and other Government and Binding syntacticians deal with coordinate structures only to a minor extent, presumably because their restriction on anaphora as it is defined in terms of c-command has nothing to say about the coreference options of NPs in such sentences. In sentences like (109a), there are no relevant c-command relations between the pronoun and the full NP, and if the anaphora rule were to be applied here, it would incorrectly predict the sentence to be grammatical.

(109) a.*_She_ decided to buy the dress, but _Leslie_ didn't.

b.

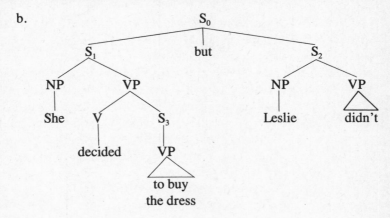

Reinhart (1983b) claims that coordinate structures are somehow special and that 'there is no reason to expect that the unavailability of anaphora in [sentences like (109), MRW] should be attributed to sentence-level considerations' (p. 55), but I consider it to be a weakness that the theory cannot account for such a fundamental sentence type as the above. I also think that the same principle that is capable of blocking coreference in (110)—which _can_ be explained in terms of c-command—should be able to account for (109) as well, since the two examples not only intuitively seem very similar, but also have much in common syntactically and thematically.

(110) a.*_She_ decided to buy the dress when _Leslie_ didn't.

b.

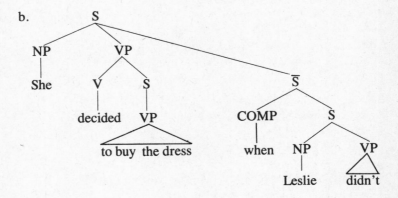

### 3.2.4  *Sentential Adverbials*

A theoretical problem related to Reinhart's structural distinction between preposed sentential and verb phrasal PPs (see 3.1.1) is mentioned by McCawley
(1984), who points out an unfortunate consequence of Reinhart's approach concerning the c-command domains of subjects. There is à priori nothing wrong
with the assumption that the structural difference between sentential and verb
phrasal PPs is maintained when preposed, but it is theoretically undesirable to
claim in the same theory—especially one which tries to completely discard the
importance of linear order—that a sentential PP (or other sentential adverbial)
has a different structural relation to the subject depending on whether it is pre-
or postposed. In the light of sentences like the following, it is necessary for
Reinhart to claim that a postposed sentential adverbial is within the scope of the
subject, while the same adverbial when preposed is not:

(111) a.\**She* rested after *Leslie* had played tennis.

b.
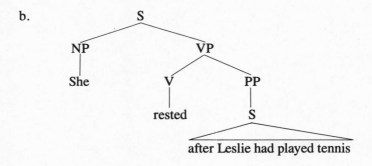

(112) a. After *Leslie* had played tennis, *she* rested.

b.
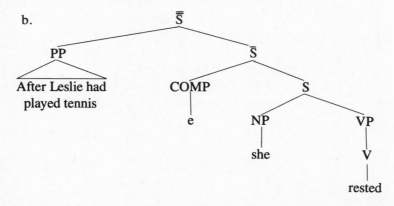

## 3.2.5  *Definiteness/Specificity*

So far in this thesis I have only discussed the coreference relationship between pronouns and *definite* NPs. The reason for this is that a purely syntactic approach to anaphora cannot account for *indefinite* NPs under the same principle, a fact which I would claim counts very much to its disadvantage. Reinhart (1983b), for example, simply says that indefinite NP anaphora seems 'to require a special, stronger condition' (p. 112) on coreference than definite NPs. That this is the case becomes clear when we consider the following two sentences, in which, of course, the syntactic tree structures are identical:

(113)   Before *he* could protest, *Peter* had been taken to court.

(114)   *Before *he* could protest, *a man* had been taken to court.

I am of the opinion, however, that this difference should be treated pragmatically, since aspects of reference as well as features such as definiteness and specificity are clearly related to the information structure of a sentence. It is also arguable that the same principle should be able to account for the equally ungrammatical (115) and (116):

(115)   **He* was taken to court before *Peter* could protest.

(116)   **He* was taken to court before *a man* could protest.

## 3.2.6  *Effects of Constituent-length and Intonation*

The final aspect of the purely syntactic analysis that I would like to criticize in this chapter concerns the effects that constituent-length and intonation may have on the coreference options of NPs in certain sentences. Both length and intonation affect the information relationships and thematic structure of the various constituents of a sentence, but not the syntactic tree.

Reinhart (1981) notes herself that some sentences with verb phrasal PPs which are ungrammatical when preposed if they contain a definite NP c-commanded by a pronoun in subject position become more acceptable when the PP is expanded:

(117)   *In *Peter's* kitchen, *he* cooks the most exotic dishes.

(118)   In *Peter's* wonderful new kitchen equipped with all kinds of modern appliances, *he* cooks the most exotic dishes.

This cannot be accounted for under Reinhart's theory unless one claims, as she in fact does, that the PP, if long, automatically becomes a sentential one and is thus attached to $\bar{\bar{S}}$ instead of its more normal position in COMP. My major objection to this solution is that length is a matter of degree, and that it is impossible to maintain a clear-cut distinction between sentential and verb phrasal PPs based on this. There are also degrees of acceptability in sentences like this, and I will later[28] argue that this is as predicted if one takes thematic structure into account in the analysis of this phenomenon.

A related problem was noted by Lakoff (1968), who cites examples like (119) and (120) to show that factors like stress and intonation, which concern the information structure of sentences, can affect the coreference options of NPs.

(119)  *Before *he* could say anything, Leslie kissed *Jóhn*.

(120)   Before *he* could say anything, Leslie kíssed *John*.

That is, when the full NP is stressed, as in (119), it cannot serve as the antecedent to the pronoun in the preposed subordinate clause, but when it is unstressed, as in (120), coreference is fine. The fact that intonation and stress can influence coreference options can be easily demonstrated by means of several of the examples given so far in this thesis[29], but as there is obviously no change in the syntactic structure, Reinhart's analysis cannot account for this either.

## 3.3   *Conclusion*

In the preceding sections of this chapter I have criticized Reinhart's account of anaphora within the Government and Binding framework. This criticism has been based on problems connected with her theory which either produce incorrect results or which are theoretically unsatisfactory. In the light of the examples I have given, I am forced to conclude that a purely syntactic approach to anaphora must be abandoned and that the answer to all the unsolved problems should be sought in a different theory of grammar. Since many of the unexplained facts involve processes which clearly have a pragmatic function, I am convinced that definite NP anaphora can best be explained in a functional theory of grammar which takes aspects like thematic structure, information relations and intonation pattern as well as discourse factors into account when analyzing linguistic phenomena.

# 4
# A Pragmatic Analysis of Anaphora

## 4.0 *Introduction*

Although the aspects of anaphora discussed in the previous chapter, in my opinion at least, clearly suggest the need for a pragmatic account of the phenomenon, not very much work has been done on anaphora in other frameworks than generative grammar. This could be due to the fact that many linguists today are skeptical of pragmatic or functional approaches. A pragmatic analysis of anaphora has also been 'proven' wrong by Reinhart (1976). Another, and perhaps more important reason, could be the prominence that is attributed to these questions in the Government and Binding framework; anaphora is considered a cornerstone of this theory and therefore possibly a problem area that other theories should 'keep their hands off'.

There are, however, certain linguists, who in spite of the generally unfavorable attitude in the field to functionalism, have made an attempt to give a pragmatic account of this problem. I think that these linguists have made important contributions to the question of anaphoric relations, and that much linguistic insight can be gained by investigating the pragmatics involved in this phenomenon. In the following section, therefore, I will briefly survey the previous research that has been done on anaphora in discourse-based models, before I embark on my own analysis of the phenomenon in the latter half of this chapter.

## 4.1 *Previous Research*

### 4.1.1 *Kuno's Analysis*

To my knowledge, Kuno (1972a and b) was the first linguist to look at anaphora from the point of view of information relationships. Although he basically adheres to Langacker's syntactic restriction of precede-and-command as well as the notion of a transformational process which operates on fully specified deep structures, Kuno also claims that there is a pragmatic principle at play, which takes into account the distinction between old, predictable information and new, unpredictable information. In this respect it is obvious that Kuno relies heavily on the theory of Functional Sentence Perspective (FSP) as formulated by Jan Firbas and other structuralists belonging to the Prague school.

Kuno's analysis can be divided into three basic hypotheses, which together with the syntactic notion of precede-and-command as well as some other discourse-based restrictions, should account for all instances of definite NP anaphora. His most important claim is represented in (121):

(121) Backward pronominalization is possible in English only when the rightmost of the two coreferential noun phrases represents old predictable information (Kuno 1972b, p. 302).

The above hypothesis, although it paradoxically enough explicitly mentions backwards pronominalization, claims that a pronoun can occur to the left of its coreferring full NP only if its referent is known from preceding context (i.e. it is really an instance of intersentential forwards pronominalization). Restriction (121) was intended for sentences like the following:

(122) a. Speaker A:   Who is visiting John?
      b. Speaker B:   *His* brother is visiting *John*.

(123) a. Speaker A:   Who is visiting who?
      b. Speaker B: **His* brother is visiting *John*.
          (Kuno 1975, p. 278).

The acceptability of (122b) is due to the fact that the referent of the pronoun *his* is determinable from the preceding context, whereas (123b), which is structurally identical, must be unacceptable since the hearer has no clue as to the reference of the pronoun (and, as I will claim later, it cannot pick up its reference from the following full NP).

Kuno's second hypothesis is represented as (124):

(124) A noun phrase that represents what the sentence is about, namely, the theme of the sentence, cannot be pronominalized intrasententially  (Kuno 1972b, p. 305).

This hypothesis was based on discourses like the following:

(125)   What did John do for Mary?
    a. When *he* went to Boston, *John* took her out to dinner.
    b.*When *John* went to Boston, *he* took her out to dinner
       (Kuno 1972b, p. 305).

That is, the ungrammaticality of (125b) is due to the fact that the underlying subject of the matrix sentence, *John,* which is also the predictable theme since it is mentioned in the preceding context, has been pronominalized with an instance of the antecedent in the same sentence.

The third hypothesis that Kuno proposes is represented in (126):

(126) Noun phrases of exhaustive listing[30] interpretation cannot be pro-nominalized intrasententially (Kuno 1972b, p. 306).

The hypothesis in (126) can be used to explain the grammaticality versus ungrammaticality of sentences like those in (127):

(127) a.  Among *John,* Mary, Jane, and Martha, *John* is the tallest.
       b.*Among *John,* Mary, Jane, and Martha, *he* is the tallest.
          (Kuno 1972b, p. 306).

Although Kuno undoubtedly made an important contribution to the existing theory of anaphora and, in my opinion, certainly is 'on the right track', it is not difficult to find fault with his analysis. Carden (1982), for example, argues convincingly against what he calls the 'Forwards-Only-Hypothesis' (and thus Kuno's first hypothesis) by providing innumerable examples of sentences like the following to show that they are completely acceptable as the beginning of a discourse:

(128) After *his* recent election as Republican national chairman, *Bill Broch* said... (Carden 1982, p. 366).[31]

### 4.1.2  *Bickerton's Analysis*

Unlike Kuno, who retains the old syntactic notion of 'primacy relations', Bickerton (1975) discards the generative framework entirely in his analysis of anaphora. He argues that syntactic relations play no role in determining the reference of pronouns, and claims that by taking three phenomena into con-sideration—presupposition/assertion, sentence stress and intersentential anaphora—it is possible to derive a single principle that will account for all cases of coreferential pronominalization. Bickerton formulates this principle in the following way:

(129) Pronominalization flows bidirectionally, and across sentence boundaries, from presupposed to asserted NP, and between presupposed NP, except where one NP has been presupposed throughout its derivational history and the other has not; in the latter case, pronominalization shall be from the more-consistently to the less-consistently presupposed (Bickerton 1975, pp. 32-33).

This principle will, for example, correctly predict the grammaticality versus ungrammaticality of the following sentences:

(130)  *What annoyed *him* was my punching *Bill*.

(131)   It was my punching *him* that annoyed *Bill*.

Both (130) and (131) can be interpreted, as is common with cleft and pseudo-cleft sentences, as consisting of a presupposed and an asserted part. In (130), the information in the *wh*-clause is presupposed and the rest of the sentence asserted, whereas in (131) it is the clefted part of the sentence which is asserted, and the information in the following relative clause which is presupposed. The data in (130) and (131) thus seem to confirm Bickerton's principle that pronominalization flows from presupposed to asserted NPs; i.e a pronoun may corefer with a full NP only if the antecedent is in the presupposed and the pronoun in the asserted part of the sentence.

It is also interesting to note here that (130) is identical in structure to one of the problematic cases for the purely syntactic account (see section 3.2.2 on ordering). Since the pronoun is not, in surface structure at least, in a syntactic position where it c-commands its antecedent, Reinhart's anaphora rule will incorrectly derive (130) as a grammatical sentence.

There are, however, other shortcomings of Bickerton's analysis, and although it seems quite convincing at first sight, it does not hold when investigated more closely. Bickerton discusses in great detail the effects of intonation and stress on the information structure of a sentence, but his analysis is nevertheless incapable of accounting for the unacceptability of the following sentence:

(132)  *$\overset{\frown}{He}$ was annoyed by the fact the I pu$\overset{\frown}{n}$ched *Bill*.

The pronoun in (132) is stressed and must therefore be interpreted as asserted material. If also the verb in the embedded clause carries stress, this will ensure the interpretation of the final NP as presupposed. According to Bickerton's principle, then, pronominalization should be able to flow from the final NP to the initial NP here (from presupposed to asserted), but as the sentence is obviously ungrammatical with coreference, Bickerton's analysis must be said to be inadequate in this respect. Sentence (132) also shows that a change in intonation and stress is not enough to create an acceptable sentence from one that is structurally unacceptable.

### 4.1.3  *Bolinger's Analysis*

Bolinger (1979) approaches the problem of pronominal anaphora from a very different viewpoint. Instead of regarding the presence of a pronoun as the result of a mechanical process triggered by a coindexed full noun, which he, incidentally, considers to be the main error of traditional treatments, Bolinger uses communicative function as his point of departure and treats the whole question of anaphora as the speaker's pragmatic choice between a nominal with rich semantic content (the full NP) and a nominal with less semantic content (the pronoun). His principle, then, which he formulates as (133), is thus not concerned with the question of when a pronoun can occur, but rather when a full NP can be used to reidentify a referent that has already been introduced into the discourse.

> (133) The topic may be reidentified easily in the theme, but in the rheme only if the theme lacks a normally topical form (subject noun or subject pronoun) (Bolinger 1979, p. 306).

The following sentences can thus be accounted for:

> (134)  The moment *he* arrived, *John* was recognizable.

> (135)  *\*He* was recognizable the moment *John* arrived.

> (136)  I recognized *him* the moment *John* arrived.
>        (Bolinger 1979, p. 306).

In (134) the reidentification, i.e. the full NP, is in the theme, and the sentence is fine with coreference as expected according to Bolinger's condition. In (135) and (136), however, the reidentification of the referent is in the rheme.

This is possible, Bolinger claims, only when the coreferring pronoun in the theme is not in topical form, i.e. when it is not the subject of the sentence. Sentence (135) is therefore correctly predicted to be ungrammatical with co-reference, while (136) is fine. This distinction thus captures the same subject/non-subject asymmetry that was noted earlier (see section 3.1.2), without the additional problems of Reinhart's syntactic analysis in terms of c-command.

Bolinger's approach is extremely interesting and seems to account for most of the sentences that are apt to crop up in analyses of pronominal anaphora. There is one type of sentence that the principle stated in (133) seems unable to account for, however. These are exactly the sentences which are so important for Reinhart's definition of c-command, namely sentences with verb phrasal and sentential PPs. When these PPs are preposed, as in (137) and (138) below, Bolinger's principle cannot account for the difference in grammaticality since it only mentions *reidentification* and thus seems to allow forwards pronominalization in an unrestricted fashion.

(137)   In *Leslie's* home town, *she* is considered a good writer.

(138)   *In *Leslie's* home town, *she* spent most of her life.

The difference in grammaticality is also visible before preposing of the PPs, as in (139) and (140), but again Bolinger's condition will interpret the two as identical. Since the reidentification is not in the theme,[32] both sentences should be grammatical since the pronouns are not subjects. Sentence (139) is correctly predicted to be grammatical, but as (140) is obviously ungrammatical, one is forced to the conclusion that Bolinger's analysis is inapplicable for sentences of this type.

(139)   They consider *her* a good writer in *Leslie's* home town.

(140)   *They let *her* spend most of her life in *Leslie's* home town.

## 4.2   *A New Pragmatic Analysis of Anaphora*

### 4.2.1   *Introduction*

After having closely investigated especially syntactic but also pragmatic approaches to definite NP anaphora, I would now like to introduce my own view of this phenomenon. As is apparent from my criticism of the various approaches, I am more inclined to accept a theory which takes account of pragmatic factors than a purely syntactic one. My own analysis is thus influenced by the scholars who have contributed to the theory of pragmatics as well as those who have specifically dealt with the problem of anaphoric relations in recent years. In the following, however, I will attempt to look at this problem from a slightly different angle.

### 4.2.2  General Framework

The linguistic framework on which I will base my analysis of anaphora is mainly that of the Prague school, as it is formulated in the work of Jan Firbas and his associates. This framework deals with language as a process of communication, and the organization of information is thus an important aspect of it. Fundamental to this theory is the notion of Communicative Dynamism (CD) which has to do with the 'extent to which [a] sentence element contributes to the development of communication, to which, as it were, it 'pushes' the communication forward' (Firbas 1966, p. 240).

The notion of CD is incorporated into a system called Functional Sentence Perspective (FSP). Firbas (1966, p. 241) states that FSP is understood as 'the distribution of degrees of CD over the elements within a sentence', and it basically assumes that sentence elements follow each other according to the amount of CD they convey, starting with the lowest and gradually passing on to the highest. The unmarked word order and the most common distribution of CD in a sentence is thus a consistent *theme-transition-rheme* sequence, illustrated by the sentence in (141):

(141) The man      baked      bread
      THEME-TRANSITION-RHEME

It is obvious, then, that linear order as well as concepts like theme/rheme, given/new and focus are important in this theory. But Firbas (1966, p. 241) also states that the 'distribution of degrees of CD over the elements in a sentence' is not merely due to pragmatics, but is rather 'the outcome of an interplay (tension)' of several factors. This model of language postulates three distinct but interrelated levels of structure: syntax, semantics, and FSP, which are all to some extent responsible for word order and other linguistic phenomena. There may therefore be both semantic and language-specific syntactic restrictions which bring about a marked word order. It will later become clear that this is fairly common in English, but the system of FSP is nevertheless quite powerful and it continuously works towards a *theme-transition-rheme* order.

### 4.2.3  *Definitions of Concepts*

Notions such as theme/rheme, topic/comment and given/new etc. have been given various definitions in the literature both by Prague linguists and others interested in the pragmatic aspects of language. A thorough outline of the history and various definitions of these concepts is given in Magretta (1977). In the present analysis of pronominal anaphora, I will make use of the following concepts: theme/rheme, unmarked/marked theme, given/ new, rheme proper and focus. The definitions that I will adopt are fairly common and mainly taken from Quirk and Greenbaum (1973), Firbas (1966), and Chafe (1976).

#### 4.2.3.1  *Theme/Rheme*

The distinction between *theme* and *rheme* is considered by some grammarians to be merely a question of linear order, while others relate it to information structure. I will adopt the former approach and claim, with Quirk and Greenbaum (1973), that the theme is 'the initial unit of a clause' (p. 411). It may thus be characterized as the 'communicative point of departure for the rest of the clause' (p. 412), and stated informally, then, the theme could be said to be the element which the rest of the sentence is about.

The rest of the sentence can be divided into a transition and a rheme. The former is usually constituted by the verb, while the latter can be characterized as any element, usually nominal, following the verb.

#### 4.2.3.2  *Unmarked/Marked Theme*

In the unmarked case, the theme in regular statements coincides with the grammatical subject, as in (142):

> (142) Leslie bought the dress
>         ↓
>     SUBJECT=
>     UNMARKED THEME

Elements other than the subject, such as complements, direct and indirect objects etc., may for various stylistic reasons be preposed and thus given thematic prominence. These elements are called marked themes. Sentence (143) represents an example of this:

(143) The apple she gave to Leslie's sister.

    ↓

    DIRECT OBJECT=
    MARKED THEME

The distinction between unmarked and marked theme is an important one in the present analysis. The reason is that although both elements carry thematic prominence, they differ in their information value; whereas unmarked themes are usually old or given information, marked themes usually carry new information, since one of the reasons for thematic fronting, or topicalization as it is also often called, is to give the fronted element not only thematic prominence but informational prominence as well.

### 4.2.3.3   *Given/New*

The distinction between *given* and *new* information is naturally related to the information structure of a sentence, but there seems to be some controversy concerning the definitions of these terms as well. In Firbas's system the terms *given* and *new* do not exist, but they are certainly related, and in some cases they directly correspond, to his theme/rheme distinction. Chafe (1976), on the other hand, defines given (or old) information as the 'knowledge which the speaker assumes to be in the consciousness of the addressee at the time of the utterance' (p. 30). I agree with Firbas's view that an element which is considered given is something that has usually been provided by previous context, while new information has not. I will, however, unlike Firbas, keep the given/new distinction separate from the concepts theme/rheme, which I have defined in terms of linear order, although the two distinctions necessarily very often coincide.

There is also much discussion on the question of whether the given/new distinction is a discrete dichotomy or a matter of degree. Chafe (1976), for example, has to take the former stand since one cannot assume information to be 'in the addressee's consciousness to a greater or lesser degree' (p. 33). I do not accept this view, and will again agree with Firbas, whose theory rests on the postulation that sentence elements can carry varying degrees of CD; a high degree of CD is associated with newness and a low degree with givenness. My reason for adopting this view is that in sentences like (144) and (145), which both express the same semantic content, the sentence element *an apple* obviously plays two different roles pragmatically, i.e. it tends to carry a higher degree of CD, and hence be 'newer', in (145). This is so in spite of the fact that both sentences could be used as the beginning of a story (although

(145) is certainly less likely in this position), in which case the whole sentence is technically new, and consequently none of the elements can be considered to have been in the consciousness of the hearer.

(144) Leslie gave *an apple* to her sister.

(145) What Leslie gave her sister was *an apple*.

It should perhaps be noted that although I adopt Firbas's view here, I recognize the fact that Chafe's theory is also capable of accounting for the difference between the above two sentences as well. To do this, he introduces the notion of *contrastiveness*, a feature that can be added to NPs either by intonation and stress or by syntactic constructions like e.g. the Pseudo-cleft in (145). Chafe argues quite convincingly for this notion, which, however, seems to be more similar to what I will simply call focus.

### 4.2.3.4  *Focus*

Focus on an element in a sentence can be achieved by intonation (stress) in the spoken language, and by certain syntactic devices, e.g. Clefting, in writing. According to Quirk and Greenbaum (1973), stress usually falls at the end of a tone group (corresponding to a clause in writing) in a normal intonation pattern, and focus thus normally coincides with the rheme and the newest element. Focus may also fall on any other element of the clause, in which case it has contrastive function. In the following, I will argue that contrastive focus does not necessarily coincide with the most rhematic[33] element of the clause; i.e. there may be several new elements, and the one bearing the highest degree of CD does not always have to be the contrastive focus.

As was noted above (section 3.2.6), intonation and stress sometimes affect the coreference options of NPs. An important question which naturally arises, then, is when and why this happens, and in the following I will therefore try to explain under which circumstances a prosodic factor like stress may be of significance for the reference options of pronouns and full NPs.

### 4.2.3.5  *Thematic/Rhematic*

In this section I have so far introduced and given my definitions of concepts like *theme/rheme*, *given/new* and *focus*, which will all be of great importance for my theory of anaphora. I believe that theme/rheme structure, information structure and focus structure are all distinct levels of analysis, but that they interact to a great extent. I will therefore use the adjectives *thematic* and *rhematic* as cover terms for the three levels when describing NPs. All NPs, then, whether they are pronouns or full NPs, can be said to be thematic or rhematic to a greater or lesser degree. The most thematic element will be an NP which is the theme of the sentence and which at the same time carries old information and has no contrastive stress, while the most rhematic element will be an NP which is rheme and which carries new information and focus simultaneously.

### 4.2.3.6  *Rheme Proper*

The terms rheme proper and theme proper are also frequently used in pragmatic theory, e.g. by Firbas (1966). I will only make use of the former in the present analysis, and give it the following definition: an element in the rheme which also bears the highest degree of CD in the sentence is the rheme proper.

### 4.2.3.7  *Grammaticality/Acceptability*

So far in this thesis I have mainly used the term ungrammatical with reference to asterisked sentences. This is due to the fact that the term is in common usage among syntacticians, and it also corresponds to their view of anaphora, namely that it is an aspect of syntax. Sentences with pronouns and full NPs can thus be divided into two categories only: those cases where the pronoun c-commands the full NP and those cases where it does not, resulting in ungrammatical and grammatical sentences respectively.

I would claim, however, that the question of anaphora can best be explained at the level of pragmatics. At this level it is more appropriate to look upon sentences as more or less acceptable, depending on context and various other factors. I will therefore in the following use the terms *acceptable* and *unacceptable* when analyzing sentences, although I will, for lack of a better and more elaborate system, still use asterisks to mark the sentences that are unacceptable.

### 4.2.4  *Outlining the Theory*

### 4.2.4.1  *General Principles*

The process of communication seems to be governed by certain general principles which affect both the theme/rheme and information structures of sentences. These are also of great importance in the choice of pronouns or full NPs in coreferring expressions. In this section, therefore, I will outline the general principles that seem to be relevant to the analysis of anaphora.

The first principle that is significant in this respect is well-known within pragmatic theory, and within Czech linguistics it is called the principle of Functional Sentence Perspective (FSP). This basically says that information relations are, in most languages, structured such that one begins the sentence with old or given information and then proceeds to newer information. For convenience this will simply be referred to as Principle A in the present theory.

>(146) *Principle A*: There is a strong tendency in English[34] to structure sentence elements linearly according to the degree of newness they convey—starting with the lowest and gradually passing on to the highest.

The next principle, which concerns the reference of pronouns, is also well known within pragmatic theory. I have chosen to formulate it as (147); what it basically says is that the referent of a pronoun must be clear from the deictic or linguistic context or from a full NP introduced in the same sentence. An important effect of this principle is that it ensures that the pronoun usually follows its coreferring full NP.

>(147) *Principle B:* A person (or thing) can be referred to by a pronoun only if it is understood by the speaker/hearer *who* (or what) is being referred to, i.e. the pronoun must in a sense convey given information.

A principle noted by Hinds (1982) concerns the cases where there is a choice between a full NP and a pronoun. I will formulate this in the following way:

>(148) *Principle C:* In a longer passage or discourse where the same referent is constantly the theme of discussion,[35] there is a choice of full NP or pronoun. When a full NP is used, this highlights the information conveyed in the sentence, while 'a pronoun is used to indicate information that is less prominent semantically' (Hinds 1982, p. 85).

Principle C may, however, in certain cases be overridden by other principles, for example the principle of economy. This is related to one of Grice's (1975) conversational maxims, which simply says:

(149) Do not make your contribution more informative than is required (Grice 1975, p. 45).

For our purposes, this can be represented as (150):

(150) *Principle D:* It is not necessary to repeat the full NP if the reference of this NP is absolutely clear also if a pronoun is used.

One of the effects of Principle D is related to the problem which Bolinger (1979) was concerned with in his analysis of anaphora, namely under what conditions a referent can be reintroduced by a full NP. Principle D captures the unlikelihood of referring to an entity by means of a full NP if it is so clear who or what is being referred to that a pronoun has been used earlier in the same sentence.

The final principle that I would like to mention here is related to yet another of Grice's maxims, namely the following:

(151) Avoid ambiguity (Grice 1975, p. 46).

Since it is obvious that the referent of a pronoun can be ambiguous,[36] and that one in many cases has a choice between a pronoun and a full NP, Principle E can be formulated in the following way:

(152) *Principle E:* If the use of a pronoun will cause ambiguity as to the reference of this NP, a semantically richer NP should be used.

### 4.2.4.2 *Two Restrictions*

I believe that the distribution of coreferential pronouns and full NPs basically follows the general principles outlined in the preceding section. But these principles only describe the most common cases and some of them may be violated, without this resulting in totally unacceptable sentences. One therefore needs some stronger restrictions to capture the unacceptability of sentences like (153), in which the pronoun precedes the full NP. But the linear order of these two constituents is not the cause of the unacceptability of this sentence, as becomes evident when one compares it to the acceptable (154).

(153) *\*She* didn't like the fact that *Leslie* was kissed.

(154) The fact that *she* was kissed didn't bother *Leslie*.[37]

Both (153) and (154) are in a sense a violation of Principle B above, since a pronoun is used before the referent has been introduced by a full NP. To capture the difference between the two sentences, then, I postulate the following restriction:

(155)   *Restriction 1*: A pronoun as unmarked theme (subject) cannot pick up its reference from a full NP in the same sentence.[38]

The second restriction that I want to introduce in this section can be illustrated by comparing (154) with the structurally identical, but informationally different, (156):

(156)   *The fact that *she* was kissed didn't bother *Leslie*.

In (156), the full NP is stressed[39] and thus made more rhematic, and the resulting sentence is unacceptable with coreference. Since the full NP in this case also conveys new information and occurs in rheme position, the following formulation for Restriction 2 can be postulated:

(157)   *Restriction 2:* A pronoun cannot pick up its reference from a full NP in the same sentence, if this NP is the rheme proper.

### 4.2.4.3   *General Tendency*

The principles and restrictions stated above suggest a general tendency for the distribution of coreferential pronouns and full NPs. Although the pronoun in a sense has to convey given information (cf. Principle B), it does not seem to be able to be *given* to a greater degree than its coreferring NP; i.e. it tends to occur in a more rhematic position. This may look like a paradox, but can be given a principled explanation based on Principles B, D, and E above.

Principle B says that the referent of a pronoun must be somehow supplied by the immediate context. If the pronoun is more thematic than a full NP in the same sentence, however, the hearer will interpret the pronoun as being given already and start searching for a referent in the previous discourse. This is the case in sentence (153) above. If one wanted the two NPs to corefer in this sentence, Principle D would come into play and say that if the referent is already known information to the extent that it can be referred to by a thematic pronoun, it is unnecessary to reintroduce him/her again by a full NP in the same sentence. According to this principle, then, sentence (153) with coreferring NPs that were both given information already would simply have the following form:

(158) *She* didn't like the fact that *she* was kissed.

### 4.2.4.4 *Formulation of a Super-principle*

The general tendency mentioned above seems to be consistent in all the examples that I have investigated (see Chapter 5). It is therefore possible to formulate it as a principle in the present theory. This principle has a different status and stands in a sense above all the other principles. While principles A–E may sometimes be violated without causing a change in coreference options of the NPs of a sentence, the present principle seems always to correspond to the acceptability of sentences: if a pronoun is less thematic than a full NP in the same sentence, the two NPs may corefer, but if the pronoun is the more thematic element, coreference is impossible. I therefore postulate it as a Super-principle in the theory, and it is thus assumed to have the same function as the anaphora rule in syntactic frameworks:

> (159) *Super-principle:* In sentences with coreferring NPs where one is a pronoun and the other a full NP, the pronoun may not be more thematic than the NP from which it picks up its reference.

This Super-principle also explains the two restrictions that were formulated above: Restriction 1, as will be recalled, says that the pronoun may not be the unmarked theme, and Restriction 2 considers sentences where the full NP is the rheme proper as unacceptable. In both these cases the Super-principle must necessarily have been violated too. That this principle is also independently needed can be shown by sentence (160). Neither Restriction 1 nor Restriction 2 is violated in this case, but the sentence is nevertheless unacceptable. The explanation here lies in the fact that the pronoun conveys more *given* information than the full NP and is thus more thematic.

> (160) *It bothered *her* that *Leslie* failed the exam.

### 4.2.4.5 *A System Based on Scalar Values*

The general tendency noted in the preceding section, formulated as the Super-principle in (159), suggests the possibility of setting up a system by which NPs are given points on a scale according to how much newness, or rather 'rhematicity' they carry. The assignment of points to a certain NP should be based on several factors and involve aspects such as position in the sentence in terms of theme/rheme structure, the degree of given/new information, as well as the question whether this NP can carry focus. When all these things have been considered, the sentence will be matched with the Super-principle, which will interpret the reference of these NPs. In the cases where a pronoun carries less points than a full NP on this scale, i.e. when it is more thematic,[40] the two will be interpreted as non-coreferential.

An important aspect of this scalar system is the claim that pronouns and full NPs must start out with a difference in values, regardless of their position in the sentence or their information value. This is due to the fact that a full NP is semantically heavier than a pronoun and thus carries more information. I therefore postulate that if a pronoun starts out with, say, the value 0, a full NP must necessarily have $+1$.

This postulation is not at all undesirable for the theory—one could rather say that it is a strong argument in its favor. The reason for this claim is that the difference in values mirrors the contradiction mentioned above; although a pronoun is at the outset more thematic than a full NP, the Super-principle will ensure that other factors in the sentence make it more rhematic for the two to corefer.

The position of an NP in a sentence in terms of theme/rheme is of course important for the assignment of points on this scale. I suggest that the theme gets one point on the negative side of the scale, while the NP which constitutes the rheme will receive one point on the positive side.

Even more important on this scale is the distinction between given and new information. According to the principle of FSP (see the formulation of Principle A in 4.2.4.1 above), this very often corresponds to and thus reinforces the theme/rheme distincion. But the difference between given and new information is sometimes also independent of this, as a new element may for example be a marked theme, the unmarked theme with contrastive stress or any other element in the rheme. The given/new distinction must therefore be kept separate from the theme/rheme distinction on the scale, and the subtraction versus addition of a point for a given or new element respectively will be totally independent of its position in the sentence.

This scalar system can thus be represented as follows:

(161) Pronoun:    0                              Full NP:    $+1$

             Theme:   $-1$
             Rheme:   $+1$
             Given:   $-1$
             New:     $+1$

Examples of how this system works are given in the following sentences:

(162) a. *Peter* didn't care about the fact that they avoided *him*.

    b. Full NP:  +1               Pronoun:    0

                       − 1  (theme)                    +1  (rheme)

                    (− 1  (given))               (+1  (new))

                        0 (−1)                     +1  (+2)

(163) a.\**He* didn't care about the fact that they avoided *Peter*.

    b. Pronoun:    0             Full NP:    +1

                       − 1  (theme)                 +1  (rheme)

                    (− 1  (given))             (+1  (new))

                       −1 (−2)                +2  (+3)

In both the above sentences, the pronouns start out at 0 points and the full NPs at +1. In (162), the full NP is theme, and thus loses a point, while the pronoun in rheme position receives one. The opposite situation holds in (163); the pronoun loses a point while the full NP receives one. In the above sentences it is difficult to say which element is new and which is given information without knowing the intonation pattern. It is reasonable to assume, however, that this corresponds to the theme/rheme distinction, as in the unmarked case. Whether one takes this into account or not, the Super-principle will nevertheless interpret the values and come to the following conclusion: in (162), the pronoun has a higher value than the full NP, and it is thus possible (indeed very likely) for the pronoun to pick up its reference from this NP. In (163), on the other hand, the pronoun has a lower value than the full NP, i.e. it is more thematic. The Super-principle will therefore determine that this sentence must be unacceptable with coreference, and the referent of the pronoun must be sought elsewhere.

The effects of intonation and stress are also an important aspect of this theory. Just about any element in a sentence can be given contrastive focus by the addition of stress. This necessarily alters the given/new distinction to a certain extent, but it does not, of course, affect theme/rheme relations. In this theory, therefore, a focused element will not automatically be considered the most rhematic element, but it will simply receive one extra point on the positive side of the scale.

This system is meant to capture the fact that stress sometimes alters the co-reference options of NPs and sometimes does not. In the former case the pronoun and full NP must have equal values in terms of thematicity before the addition of stress, which will, in case it is assigned to the full NP, cause the pronoun to be more thematic. In the latter case there are two possibilities; either the pronoun is in such a position in the sentence that it already has sufficient points on the plus side of the scale for the addition of one point to the full NP not to matter, or the pronoun is so thematic that the addition of a single point is not enough to 'save' the sentence. Examples of all three cases[41] are given in (164)-(166):

(164) a. The fact that they avoided *him* didn't bother *Peter*.

b. Pronoun:     0              Full NP:    +1

                                            +1  (rheme)

        +1  (new)                           −1  (given)

        ‾‾‾‾‾‾‾‾                             ‾‾‾‾‾‾‾‾

        +1                                  +1

c.*The fact that they avoided *him* didn't bother *Péter*.

d. Pronoun:                    Full NP:    +1  (focus)

        +1                                 ‾‾‾‾‾‾‾‾‾‾

                                           +2

(165) a. *Peter* didn't care about the fact that they avoided *him*.

b. Full NP:     0              Pronoun:   +1  (see (162))

c. *Péter* didn't care about the fact that they avoided *him*.

d. Full NP:    +1  (focus)     Pronoun:

        ‾‾‾‾‾‾‾‾‾‾

        +1                                 +1

(166) a.**He* didn't care about the fact that they avoided *Peter*.

b. Pronoun:    −1              Full NP:   +2  (see (163))

c.**Hé* didn't care about the fact that they avoided *Peter*.

d. Pronoun:    +1  (focus)     Full NP:

        ‾‾‾‾‾‾‾‾‾‾

        0                                  +2

I will end this section with a note of caution concerning this scalar system. I do not claim that it is psychologically real, nor that it should have any special status in linguistic theory. It is also possible that it should be refined so as to differentiate between degrees of newness as well as positions like embedded themes and rhemes versus 'regular' ones in order to be able to account for all the fine nuances of acceptability. I do, however, find that a scalar system is a useful tool and that it is a good way of representing the facts. The reasons for this are the following: Firstly, the system rests on certain well-known principles and can thus give a theoretical explanation of the facts, which a syntactic analysis is not capable of (there is no principled reason why speakers should internalize a definition of c-command rather than, say, command). Secondly, a scalar system mirrors the fact that there are degrees of thematicity as well as degrees of acceptability, and to a certain extent the discrepancy in values corresponds proportionally to the acceptability versus unacceptability of the sentences. Thirdly, the scalar system captures the contradiction mentioned above that although pronouns must in a sense convey given information, they cannot be more thematic than the full NP from which they pick up their reference. The fourth and final argument that can be adduced in favor of this system has also been mentioned above, namely the fact that it is capable of explaining under which circumstances prosodic factors such as intonation and stress can affect the coreference options of NPs.

# 5
# Testing the Hypothesis

## 5.0 *Introduction*

In this chapter I would like to test the hypothesis that was outlined in the preceding chapter against a purely syntactic analysis of anaphora. I will focus my attention on technical matters as well as on more theoretical aspects of the two theories. Finally, I will concentrate on some areas where a syntactic analysis is inapplicable, but where the present theory can give a satisfactory account of the coreference facts of pronouns and full NPs.

## 5.1 *Technical Aspects*

### 5.1.1 *Regular Precede-and-Command Sentences*

Sentences which were used by Langacker and other syntacticians in the earlier versions of generative grammar to argue in favor of the precede-and-command condition on anaphora were given in section 2.2 above (sentences (22)—(25)) and are repeated below for convenience. To show that the present theory may also account for these data, the (b) versions represent an analysis in terms of scalar values.

(167) a. *Leslie* liked the man who kissed *her*.

b. Full NP: $+1$              Pronoun:     $0$

           $-1$ (theme)                  $+1$ (rheme)

           $\underline{-1 \text{ (given)}}$            $\underline{+1 \text{ (new)}}$

            $-1$                   $+2$

(168) a.  The man who liked *Leslie* kissed *her*.

b.  Full NP:    +1                    Pronoun:    0
                                                  +1  (rheme)
                −1  (given)                       +1  (new)
                ───────                           ───────
                0                                 +2

c.  The man who liked *Léslie* kissed *her*.

d.  Full NP:    +1  (focus)           Pronoun:
                ───────
                +1                                +2

(169) a.*She liked the man who kissed *Leslie*.

b.  Pronoun:    0                     Full NP:    +1
                −1  (theme)                       +1  (rheme)
                −1  (given)                       +1  (new)
                ───────                           ───────
                −2                                +3

c.*Shé liked the man who kissed *Leslie*.

d.  Pronoun:    +1  (focus)           Full NP:
                ───────
                −1                                +3

(170) a.*The man who kissed *her* liked *Léslie*.[42]

b.  Pronoun:    0                     Full NP:    +1
                                                  +1  (rheme)
                −1  (given)                       +1  (new)
                ───────                           ───────
                −1                                +3

c.  The man who kissed her liked Léslie.

d.  Pronoun:    +1  (new)             Full NP:    −1  (given)
                ───────                           ───────
                +1                                +1

A sentence like (167) represents the ultimate goal of the general principles sketched above, and it is thus the most unmarked case: the full NP is the most thematic element (it is in theme position and conveys given information), while the pronoun is the most rhematic. Sentence (169), on the other hand, violates most of the principles—accordingly, the sentence is unacceptable. Both (168) and (170) illustrate intermediate cases, and I would claim that the former is on the 'right' side of the acceptability scale while the latter is not. In (168), the pronoun is the rheme and it also conveys new information, and it is thus more rhematic than the full NP; as shown in (168c), not even contrastive stress can alter that, and the sentence must be considered acceptable no matter what the intonation pattern is. The structure in (170), however, is dependent on stress for its acceptability: if the final NP is stressed and consequently understood as new information, the pronoun will be interpreted as more thematic, and the sentence is thus unacceptable with coreference. If, on the other hand, stress is shifted to the verb, the final NP will be interpreted as given information and hence as an element from which the pronoun can pick up its reference.

## 5.1.2   Sentences Explained in Terms of C-command

### 5.1.2.1   Preposed PPs

Reinhart's (1976, 1983b) argumentation against the precede-and-command restriction and in favor of her own c-command condition on anaphora is mainly based on sentences with preposed PPs. When analyzing these sentences, which are very dubious as to their acceptability in the first place, Reinhart has to introduce an extended definition of c-command (see Chapter 3), which unfortunately is not consistent with the definition that is needed in certain other cases within the Government and Binding theory.

In her analysis of preposed PPs, Reinhart (1983b) also has to make reference to pragmatic phenomena. She admits (p. 59) that there are 'certain correlations between syntactic domains and functional relations in these cases', and she in fact claims that 'in many cases the syntactic position of a PP depends crucially upon the interpretation given to the sentence'. What she means by this is that in the somewhat puzzling examples like (62) and (63), repeated below as (171) and (172), the position of the PP in the syntactic tree depends on whether it can be interpreted as given or new information. There is general agreement among linguists that sentential PPs usually convey given information while verb phrasal PPs convey new information.[43] In (172), therefore, where the PP is considered part of the new information conveyed by the sentence, it must consequently also be verb phrasal and be attached to $\overline{S}$ in COMP. In (171), on the other hand, the PP conveys given information, and the attachment of this element to a higher projection of S $(\overline{\overline{S}})$ ensures that it falls outside the scope of the subject, and coreference is thus possible.

(171)  In *Peter's* home town, *he* is still considered a good actor.

(172)  *In *Peter's* home town, *he* spent most of his life.

In my analysis the possible syntactic difference between the two PPs is disregarded and the degree of thematicity assumed to be sufficient to capture the difference in acceptability. In (171) the PP conveys given information, and the sentence can be said to follow the principle of FSP. It is thus normal to have sentential PPs in this position, and certain linguists, e.g. Kuno (1975), suggest that such PPs actually originate in initial position and are never pre-posed. The PP in (172), on the other hand, will tend to be interpreted as new information, and the sentence therefore violates the principle of FSP. This alone is not enough, however, to account for the unacceptability of this sentence (it *is* acceptable when the pronoun and full NP switch places); rather one must look at the degree of thematicity associated with each NP. In terms of scalar values this can be represented as (173b) and (174b).

(173) a.  In *Peter's* home town, *he* is still considered a good actor.

b.  Full NP:    $+1$                    Pronoun:    $0$

$$\frac{-1 \ \text{(given)}}{0} \qquad \frac{\begin{array}{l} -1 \ \text{(theme)} \\ +1 \ \text{(new)} \end{array}}{0}$$

(174) a.*In *Peter's* home town, *he* spent most of his life.

b.  Full NP:    $+1$                    Pronoun:    $0$

$$\frac{+1 \ \text{(new)}}{+2} \qquad \frac{\begin{array}{l} -1 \ \text{(theme)} \\ -1 \ \text{(given)} \end{array}}{-2}$$

In (174) the pronoun and the full NP carry very different degrees of thematicity, and since the pronoun is the more thematic element, i.e. it has a lower value on the scale than the full NP, the sentence is correctly predicted to be unacceptable in my system. The two NPs in (173) are identical in their degree of thematicity, and the sentence is thus fine with coreference. The newness of the pronoun can here be said to moderate its unfavorable starting position in terms of values on the scale.

The effect of stress in these cases may be adduced as yet another argument in support of my hypothesis. If the pronoun is stressed in (173), the coreference options do not change. In the present system, this simply makes the pronoun more rhematic and the sentence possibly more acceptable. If the full NP is stressed, however, this element suddenly becomes more rhematic, and since the two NPs had equal values previously, the Super-principle is violated. The result of this process is therefore an unacceptable sentence:

(175) a. *In $\overset{\frown}{Peter}$'s home town, *he* is still considered a good actor.[44]

b. Full NP:      0                    Pronoun:    0  (see (173))

$$\frac{+1 \ \ (focus)}{+1} \qquad\qquad 0$$

A similar result is achieved when stress is applied to the NPs in (174). Stress on the full NP in this sentence simply makes the discrepancy in values greater and thus cannot alter the coreference facts. Stress on the pronoun in this case, however, creates a sentence that is perhaps not very likely, but nevertheless one that is acceptable.

(176) a. In *Peter*'s home town, $\overset{\frown}{he}$ spent most of his life.[45]

b. Full NP:   +1                     Pronoun:    0
                                                 −1  (theme)
$$\frac{-1 \ \ (given)}{0} \qquad \frac{\begin{array}{l}+1 \ \ (new)\\ +1 \ \ (focus)\end{array}}{+1}$$

Unlike Reinhart's purely syntactic analysis, this pragmatic system can also account for the fact that the coreference options of the NPs in these sentences do not change when the pronoun is no longer the subject of the main clause. Sentences like (75) and (76), discussed in Chapter 3 and repeated here as (177) and (178), can be given the following scalar representations:

(177) a. In *Peter*'s home town, they still consider *him* a good actor.

b. Full NP:   +1                     Pronoun:    0
$$\frac{-1 \ \ (given)}{0} \qquad\qquad \frac{+1(new)}{+1}$$

c. In $\overset{\frown}{Peter}$'s home town, they still consider *him* a good actor.[46]

d. Full NP:   +1  (focus)            Pronoun:
$$\frac{}{+1} \qquad\qquad\qquad +1$$

(178) a.*In *Peter's* home town, they let *him* spend most of his life.

b.  Full NP:    +1                     Pronoun:     0
                +1  (new)                            -1  (given)
                ————                                 ————
                +2                                   -1

c.  In *Peter's* home town, they let *hím* spend most of his life.

d.  Full NP:                           Pronoun:    +1  (focus)
                -1  (given)                         +1  (new)
                ————                                ————
                 0                                   +2

As mentioned in Chapter 3, the difference in acceptability between sentences with verb phrasal and sentential PPs is visible also before preposing. Sentences (179) and (180) show that the present system may account for these cases as well.

(179) a.  They still consider *him* a good actor in *Peter's* home town.

b.  Pronoun:    0                      Full NP:    +1
                +1  (new)                          -1  (given)
                ————                               ————
                +1                                  0

c.  They still consider *hím* a good actor in *Peter's* home town.

d.  Pronoun:    +1  (focus)            Full NP:
                ————
                +2                                  0

e.*They still consider *him* a good actor in *Péter's* home town.

f.  Pronoun:                           Full NP:    +1  (focus)
                -1  (given)                         +1  (new)
                ————                               ————
                -1                                  +2

(180) a.*They let *him* spend most of his life in *Peter's* home town.

b.  Pronoun:    0                      Full NP:    +1
                -1  (given)                        +1  (new)
                ————                               ————
                -1                                  +2

c.*They let *him* spend most of his life in *Peter's* home town.

d. Pronoun: Full NP: +1 (focus)

$$-1 \qquad\qquad \frac{}{+3}$$

e.*They let *him* spend most of his life in *Peter's* home town.[47]

f. Pronoun: +1 (focus) Full NP:

$$0 \qquad\qquad\qquad +2$$

The subject/non-subject asymmetry that is present in examples of this kind may also be explained in this theory, and sentences (181) and (182), which have the pronoun in subject and thus unmarked theme position, show that this can be done by reference to the theme/rheme distinction. Compare the following sentences with (179) and (180) above:

(181) a.*He* is still considered a good actor in *Peter's* home town.

b. Pronoun: 0 Full NP: +1
$$\frac{\begin{array}{l}-1 \text{ (theme)} \\ -1 \text{ (given)}\end{array}}{-2} \qquad \frac{-1 \qquad \text{(given)}}{0}$$

c.*He* is still considered a good actor in *Peter's* home town.

d. Pronoun: +1 (focus) Full NP:
$$\frac{}{-1} \qquad\qquad\qquad 0$$

(182) a.*He* spent most of his life in *Peter's* home town.

b. Pronoun: 0 Full NP: +1
$$\frac{\begin{array}{l}-1 \text{ (theme)} \\ -1 \text{ (given)}\end{array}}{-2} \qquad \frac{+1 \text{ (new)}}{+2}$$

c.*He* spent most of his life in *Peter's* home town.

d. Pronoun: +1 (focus) Full NP:
$$\frac{}{-1} \qquad\qquad\qquad +2$$

### 5.1.2.2    *The Effects of Length and Intonation*

Throughout this pragmatic account of anaphora the effects of intonation are incorporated into the general analysis, as I attempt to investigate the conditions under which stress may or may not alter the coreference options of NPs. Wherever it is relevant, focus, and thus one extra point on the scale, is added to the NPs of a sentence after the general analysis in terms of theme/rheme and information structure has been completed.

As was noted in Chapter 3, the length of a PP may also affect the acceptability of sentences like those discussed in the preceding section. In a sentence like (172), for example, where a verb phrasal PP is preposed, coreference is blocked between the pronoun and the full NP—in my analysis because the pronoun is more thematic than the full NP, in a syntactic analysis because it c-commands this NP. When lengthened, Reinhart claims, this PP suddenly becomes sentential, and it is thus no longer in the c-command domain of the subject. I will argue, however, that it is rather the case that the length of the PP affects its value in terms of given or new information: the longer the PP, the more likely it is that it will be interpreted as 'setting the scene' for the rest of the sentence. Sentence (183), which is identical to (172) except for the fact that the PP is long, will therefore be analyzed in the following way:

(183) a.  In *Peter's* beautiful little home town up in the mountains, *he* spent most of his life.

b.  Full NP:    $+1$                              Pronoun:    $0$
                                                            $-1$ (theme)
                $\underline{-1 \text{ (given)}}$           $\underline{+1 \text{ (new)}}$
                $0$                                         $0$

In this connection I would also like to mention the fact that it is not only the length of the PP that may affect its interpretation and thus the reference options of the NPs. This change may also be effected by other factors, e.g. the structure of the following clause. In sentence (184b), for example, the simple addition of an adverbial in the main clause gives exactly the same result. While (184a) expresses where the person in question (the theme) spent his life, namely in Peter's home town, which is considered new information, (184b) tells us what happened in Peter's home town, namely that he spent his life alone there. The PP in this case is therefore understood as 'setting the scene', and thus as given information.

(184) a.*In *Peter's* home town, *he* spent most of his life.

    b. In *Peter's* home town, *he* spent most of his life alone.

In his discussion of existential sentences, Bolinger (1977) draws a similar conclusion as to the function of preposed locatives. He argues (p. 100) that although it 'may seem strange to consider a locative as topic of a sentence', the acceptability of sentences like (184b) must nevertheless be accounted for by the fact that it 'tells us something about' this preposed locative.

### 5.1.2.3 *Subjacency*

The sentences which Reinhart uses to 'prove' that the anaphora rule obeys subjacency (see section 3.1.4) can now be explained in the present theory in terms of what was said in the preceding section about length. The following two sentences, (185) and (186), differ only in the respect that the full NP in the latter is embedded in a relative clause. I will argue that the possibility of co-reference in (186) is not necessarily due to the embedding of the full NP, but rather to the fact that the additional relative clause expands the PP and thus makes it more 'given'. These sentences can therefore be interpreted in the same fashion as (184a) and (184b) above: while (185) expresses where the referent of the pronoun found a snake, (186) tells us what happened at this location. Accordingly, the PP in the former sentence is considered new information, and the PP in the latter is again conceived of as 'setting the scene' for the action, and consequently as more 'given'.

(185) a.*Near *Peter*, *he* found a snake.

    b. Full NP: $+1$            Pronoun:   $0$

                                              $-1$ (theme)

            $+1$ (new)                 $-1$ (given)

             $+2$                          $-2$

(186) a. Near the garage that *Peter* had built, *he* found a snake.

    b. Full NP: $+1$            Pronoun:   $0$

                                              $-1$ (theme)

            $-1$ (given)              $+1$ (new)

             $0$                           $0$

The present account of the facts also avoids the weakness that is inherent in Reinhart's analysis; namely that if one accepts subjacency as an explanation for the difference in acceptability of (185) and (186), one is unable to account for the subject/non-subject asymmetry that one finds in this type of sentence as well. According to Reinhart's analysis the following sentences, (187) and (188), should be equally acceptable. Sentence (188), however, where the pronoun is in subject position, is unacceptable with coreference. In the present analysis this is simply due to a violation of the Super-principle, as the pronoun is more thematic than the full NP.

(187) a.  They locked *him* into the garage that *Peter* had built.

b.  Pronoun:      0            Full NP:    +1
    $$\frac{+1 \quad \text{(new)}}{+1}$$                    $$\frac{-1 \quad \text{(given)}}{0}$$

c. *They locked *him* into the garage that *Péter* had built.[48]

d.  Pronoun:                   Full NP:    +1  (focus)
    $$\frac{-1 \quad \text{(given)}}{-1}$$                 $$\frac{+1 \quad \text{(new)}}{+3}$$

(188) a. **He* was locked into the garage that *Peter* had built.

b.  Pronoun:      0            Full NP:    +1
              -1  (theme)
    $$\frac{-1 \quad \text{(given)}}{-2}$$                 $$\frac{-1 \quad \text{(given)}}{0}$$

c. *Hé* was locked into the garage that *Peter* had built.

d.  Pronoun:  $$\frac{+1 \quad \text{(focus)}}{-1}$$    Full NP:

                                                            0

### 5.1.2.4  *Other 'Problematic' PPs*

The type of PP that is problematic for Reinhart's analysis (see section 3.1.3) is represented in sentence (189), where the anaphora rule seems to disregard the presence of the preposition. As will be recalled, Reinhart has to postulate a prepositionless NP as indirect object in underlying structure. This type of PP does not even present a problem for a pragmatic account of anaphora, since only the thematic value of an element is considered and not its position in the syntactic structure. A sentence like (189) will therefore be analyzed in exactly the same way as (190), where there is no preposition present, but where the information structure is identical to that of (189). According to the present analysis, then, both sentences are considered unacceptable with coreference since the pronoun is more thematic than the full NP.

(189) a.*It didn't occur to *her* that *Leslie* failed the exam.

b. Pronoun:    0                Full NP:   +1
               −1  (given)                 +1  (new)
               ――――――                      ――――――
               −1                           +2

(190) a.*It didn't bother *her* that *Leslie* failed the exam.

b. Pronoun:    0                Full NP:   +1
               −1  (given)                 +1  (new)
               ――――――                      ――――――
               −1                           +2

## 5.1.2.5  *Possessive NPs*

Sentences with possessive NPs have been a persistent problem for syntactic analyses of anaphora, mainly because of their very dubious grammaticality. In section 3.2.1.2 it was demonstrated that Reinhart needs two different definitions of c-command to account for sentences of the type represented in (191) below, while I argued that the difference in grammaticality judgements is dependent on whether or not one is able to construct a situation where the sentence is pragmatically plausible.

(191) ?*His* brother is visiting *John*.

Kuno (1975) provides two different contexts for this sentence, one in which it is fine with coreference between the full NP and the possessive pronoun and one where it is totally unacceptable in this reading. Kuno's examples are repeated below, together with an analysis of them in terms of scalar representations:

(192) a. Who is visiting John?

b. *His* brother is visiting *John*.

c. Pronoun:     0                Full NP:   +1

| Pronoun | Full NP |
|---|---|
| 0 | +1 |
| +1 (new) | +1 (rheme) |
| | −1 (given) |
| +1 | +1 |

d. *\*His* brother is visiting *Jo͠hn*.

| Pronoun | Full NP |
|---|---|
| | +1 (focus) |
| +1 | +2 |

(193) a. Who is visiting who?

b. *\*His* brother is visiting *John*.

c. Pronoun:     0                Full NP:   +1

| Pronoun | Full NP |
|---|---|
| 0 | +1 |
| | +1 (rheme) |
| +1 (new) | +1 (new)[49] |
| +1 | +3 |

d. *\*H͠is* brother is visiting *John*.

| Pronoun | Full NP |
|---|---|
| +1 (focus) | |
| +2 | +3 |

The context provided by (192a) ensures the interpretation of this sentence which is represented in (192c); the possessive NP is the real answer to the question and therefore the newest element, while the full NP has been mentioned already and is thus considered given information. This creates a balance of thematicity in the two NPs of the sentence as they have equal values, namely +1. If the full NP is focused, however, this balance is disturbed, and since the result of this is a pronoun which is more thematic than the full NP, the two may not corefer. Sentence (192d) is of course also totally unacceptable as an answer to the question in (192a) in any case.

The sentence in (193a), on the other hand, is a question asking for a double answer, and both NPs in (193b) must therefore be considered new information. This leads to an interpretation where the full NP is less thematic than the pronoun, and in this reading the sentence is unacceptable with coreference. (193d) represents an attempt to change the information structure of this sentence by stressing, and thereby focusing, the pronoun. This makes the pronoun more rhematic, but as is apparent from the scalar analysis in (193c), this is not sufficient to 'save' the sentence.

## 5.2   Theoretical Aspects of the Pragmatic Theory

### 5.2.1   Subject/Non-subject Asymmetry

The fact that the subject has a somewhat special status in the structure of a sentence has been acknowledged by linguists since the beginning of the study of language. I recognize, of course, the importance of the subject as a syntactic category. But just like Halliday (1970), who speaks of 'logical subjects', I want to claim that it also has a special status in terms of communication. The subject generally coincides with the unmarked theme, and this special status may thus be captured in a theory based on pragmatics as well—a fact which is not undesirable since it is fairly common for syntax and pragmatics to interact and reinforce each other. Givon (1979), for example, argues very strongly for the 'fundamental unity of language structure and language function' (p. xvii).

The unmarked theme is the element which the rest of the sentence 'is about'. In the following example, the sentence can be said to express something *about* the NP *Peter*, which is the unmarked theme in this case.

(194) Peter is an idiot.

Even when (194) is uttered completely out of context, i.e. in a situation where everything conveyed by the sentence is technically new information, it would still be understood as first introducing Peter and then saying something about this person. The unmarked theme thus very often coincides with given information, in which case this element will be the most thematic one in the sentence according to my analysis of thematicity.

When other sentence elements than the subject are preposed for thematic prominence, e.g. complements or objects, and thereby have the status of marked theme in a pragmatic analysis, they never coincide with given information. Rather, this fronting involves prominence also informationally, and the theme must in these cases be considered new information. In (195), the theme, which is a preposed object, also conveys new information, and may thus never be as thematic as the unmarked theme, i.e. the subject.

(195) Peter I like to kiss.

With this in mind, one may go on to consider the type of sentence with definite NP anaphora where there is a subject/non-subject asymmetry present (see section 3.1.2). Examples like the following, which crop up frequently in syntactic analyses, illustrate this phenomenon; and in the (b) versions of these sentences it is demonstrated that a pragmatic analysis may account for this in terms of the distinctions theme/rheme and given/new.

(196) a.  They still consider *him* a good actor in *Peter's* home town.

    b. Pronoun:     0                Full NP:   +1

$$\begin{array}{ll} 0 & +1 \\ \underline{+1 \text{ (new)}} & \underline{-1 \text{(given)}} \\ +1 & 0 \end{array}$$

(197) a.*He* is still considered a good actor in *Peter's* home town.

$$\begin{array}{ll} \text{Pronoun:}\quad 0 & \text{Full NP:}\quad +1 \\ -1 \text{ (theme)} & \\ \underline{-1 \text{ (given)}} & \underline{-1 \text{ (given)}} \\ -2 & 0 \end{array}$$

(198) a.  *Him* they consider a good actor in *Peter's* home town.[50]

$$\begin{array}{ll} \text{Pronoun:}\quad 0 & \text{Full NP:}\quad +1 \\ -1 \text{ (theme)} & \\ \underline{+1 \text{ (new)}} & \underline{-1 \text{ (given)}} \\ 0 & 0 \end{array}$$

Sentences like (196) and (197) have been accounted for above and the difference between them explained in terms of the thematicity of the pronoun; in (196) it is new information, while in (197) it is the unmarked theme and thus normally given information.[51] In (198) the pronoun also functions as theme, but since this is a marked theme, it is also necessarily new information, and the two distinctions cancel each other out. In such a sentence, therefore, the pronoun will not be more thematic than the full NP (as long as the latter element is part of a sentential PP conveying given information, of course). Coreference between the two NPs in (198) is thus possible as expected in my theory.

    The conclusion here must therefore be that a pragmatic theory may account for the well-known subject/non-subject asymmetry by taking into consideration not only the distinction between elements constituting the theme and the rheme of a sentence, but also the given/new distinction as it affects these elements and makes it possible to distinguish between marked and unmarked themes.

## 5.2.2  *Ordering*

In the various syntactic analyses of anaphora, there is one problem that seems to recur constantly, namely that of ordering. Regardless of whether one considers the rule as a transformation applying in the syntactic component or as an interpretive rule in the semantic component, one does not get rid of this problem. It is interesting to note, however, that all the transformations that pose this ordering problem when they interact with the anaphora rule are transformations that involve a change in theme/rheme structure or informational relations, such as Extraposition, Passive, Topicalization, Clefting, Adverb Preposing etc.

In the present pragmatic approach to anaphora, this ordering problem is non-existent. The anaphora rule, now formulated as the Super-principle in (159), applies to surface structures[52] only, and it thus needs no access to the derivational history of a sentence from deep structure. The rule simply applies to the phonetic form[53] of the sentence, interpreting the reference of the pronouns in the following way: if a pronoun is more thematic than a full NP in the same sentence, it must refer to some other appropriate NP which has been mentioned in previous discourse or which can be understood from immediate context. In the case where a pronoun is less thematic than the full NP, the rule will determine that the pronoun may or may not pick up its reference from this NP. Whether it actually does will of course depend on the context in each case.

In this section, therefore, I will first consider sentences that have undergone various types of transformations and see how my theory fares with respect to these. I will then go on to the sentences that are still problematic for Reinhart's approach and try to demonstate that my theory will account for those as well.

### 5.2.2.1  *Pronominalization and Extraposition*

Ross (1969) showed that in certain cases, Pronominalization could go both forwards and backwards, as e.g. in (199) and (200) below:

(199)   That *Peter* was unpopular didn't disturb *him*.

(200)   That *he* was unpopular didn't disturb *Peter*.

If these sentences also undergo Extraposition, only the one corresponding to (200), i.e. (202), where the full NP precedes the pronoun, is acceptable with coreference.

(201)   *It didn't disturb *him* that *Peter* was unpopular.

(202)   It didn't disturb *Peter* that *he* was unpopular.

The reason why (201) is unacceptable, while its source, (199), is fine with coreference, can in the present theory be explained in the following way: in (199) the pronoun is the rheme and presumably also new information, and compared with the full NP, which is not in rheme position, the pronoun cannot be considered more thematic. The Super-principle is thus not violated, and the sentence is acceptable in the interpretation that the two NPs refer to the same entity. In (201), on the other hand, the pronoun *is* more thematic than the full NP because it precedes it and should therefore be considered more given (according to the principle of FSP). An analysis of the two sentences[54] in terms of scalar values is given in (203) and (204).

(203) a.  That *Peter* was unpopular didn't disturb *him*.

    b.  Full NP:   +1               Pronoun:    0

$$\begin{array}{ll} \text{Full NP:} \quad +1 & \text{Pronoun:} \quad 0 \\ & \qquad\qquad +1 \ \text{(rheme)} \\ \underline{+1 \ \text{(new)}} & \underline{+1 \ \text{(new)}} \\ +2 & \qquad\qquad +2 \end{array}$$

    c. *That *Peter* was unpopular didn't disturb *him*.

    d.  Full NP:

$$\begin{array}{ll} \text{Full NP:} \quad \underline{+1 \ \text{(focus)}} & \text{Pronoun:} \\ \qquad\qquad +3 & \qquad\qquad +2 \end{array}$$

(204) a. *It didn't disturb *him* that *Peter* was unpopular.

    b.  Pronoun:

$$\begin{array}{ll} \text{Pronoun:} \quad 0 & \text{Full NP:} \quad +1 \\ \underline{-1 \ \text{(given)}} & \underline{+1 \ \text{(new)}} \\ \qquad -1 & \qquad\qquad +2 \end{array}$$

c. *It didn't disturb *hím* that *Peter* was unpopular.

d. Pronoun: $\dfrac{+1 \text{ (focus)}}{0}$      Full NP: $+2$

The effects of stress assigned to one of the NPs in the above sentences are represented in (203c) and (204c). In the latter sentence, the addition of focus to the pronoun cannot alter the coreference options of the two NPs, while in the former, the assignment of stress to the full NP makes this element more rhematic and thus causes a violation of the Super-principle. Accordingly, sentence (203c) is unacceptable.

### 5.2.2.2 *Pronominalization and Passive*

The Passive transformation has approximately the same effect as Extraposition, i.e. it turns material in theme position into the rheme and vice versa. Sentence (205) below is an active sentence, while (206) is the same sentence after it has undergone the Passive transformation. The former is acceptable, but the latter is unacceptable with coreference between the pronoun and the full NP. The explanation for this is unproblematic in the present theory of anaphora: in (205), the pronoun is in rheme position and therefore less thematic than the full NP, while in (206), where it constitutes the theme of the sentence, the pronoun must necessarily be more thematic. The difference in acceptability between the two sentences can thus be accounted for by reference to the Super-principle.

(205) a. That *Leslie* won the prize surprised *her*.

b. Full NP: $+1$      Pronoun: $0$
                                                         $+1$ (rheme)

         $\dfrac{+1 \text{ (new)}}{+2}$          $\dfrac{+1 \text{ (new)}}{+2}$

c. *That *Léslie* won the prize surprised *her*.

d. Full NP: $\dfrac{+1 \text{ (focus)}}{+3}$      Pronoun: $+2$

(206) a.*_She_ was surprised by the fact that _Leslie_ won the prize.

   b.  Pronoun:     0                    Full NP:    +1

                   −1  (theme)
                   −1  (given)                       +1  (new)
                   _____                           _____
                    −2                                +2

   c.*_She_ was surprised by the fact that _Leslie_ won the prize.

   d.  Pronoun:  +1  (focus)            Full NP:

                 +1  (new)
                 _____
                  +1                                  +2

The effects of stress in these sentences are shown in (205c) and (206c). The coreference options of the two NPs in the latter sentence are not affected by the the addition of stress at all; since the discrepancy in values is so great, the assignment of stress to the pronoun is not enough to make it as rhematic as the full NP. In (205c), on the other hand, the NPs have equal values, and the addition of one point to the full NP causes a violation of the Super-principle, and the result is therefore an unacceptable sentence.

### 5.2.2.3   _Pronominalization and_ there-_Insertion_

The sentences which in the Standard Theory become unacceptable because of the interaction of the transformations Pronominalization and _there_-Insertion, like e.g. (207) below, can now be easily explained in the syntactic analysis of anaphora (see section 2.5).

(207) *_A woman_ hoped that there would be _she_ elected.

Since pronouns are assumed to be derived already at deep structure in the current version of generative syntax, (207) must be considered ungrammatical not because Pronominalization has applied (it has not, in fact), but because _there_-Insertion has applied inappropriately. In the present pragmatic theory, a similar approach has to be taken: the unacceptability of the sentence is not due to the Super-principle or any other pragmatic principle concerning anaphora, but rather to an improper use of the presentative particle _there_, which, as may be recalled, normally only occurs with indefinite NPs.

#### 5.2.2.4 *The Transformations PP Preposing and Pseudo-clefting*

The types of sentences which Reinhart's syntactic analysis of anaphora cannot account for are sentences with pronouns and full NPs which have undergone the transformations PP Preposing or Pseudo-clefting. These were discussed in section 3.2.2, and the examples are repeated below for convenience. In (208) as well as in (209), the pronoun does not c-command its antecedent, and a syntactic analysis will therefore incorrectly predict both to be grammatical.

(208) *In *Peter's* apartment, we think *he* smokes pot.

(209) *What *she* believes is that *Leslie* is irresistible.

Sentences like (208), which are derived by PP Preposing, have already been shown to be analyzable in the present theory (see section 5.1.2.1) and will therefore not be discussed here. A sentence like (209) can also be easily explained in a pragmatic analysis of anaphora. The Pseudo-cleft construction creates a sentence consisting of a *wh*-clause which must be considered given information, and a main clause which conveys new information (cf. Bickerton's (1975) distinction between presupposed and asserted material in such sentences). An analysis of this sentence in terms of scalar values will therefore look like the following:

(210) a.*What *she* believes is that *Leslie* is irresistible.

| b. Pronoun: | 0 | Full NP: | +1 |
|---|---|---|---|
| | −1 (given) | | +1 (new) |
| | −1 | | +2 |

#### 5.2.3 *Sentential Adverbials and Linear Order*

In section 3.2.4 I discussed the paradox that is involved in Reinhart's analysis of anaphora concerning the status of sentential adverbials in relation to the subject: although she claims that linear order is of no importance in a syntactic theory, Reinhart is forced to conclude that a sentential adverbial *is* in the scope of the subject when postposed, while it falls outside this domain when it is preposed. This paradox is avoided in the present theory, where linear order is accounted for in terms of the position of an NP as the theme or the rheme of a sentence. The PPs in the following two sentences are thus different in thematic status; in (211) the PP functions as an element 'setting the scene' for the content that is expressed in the rest of the clause, while in (212) it is the rheme of the sentence. Its most important effect, however, is on the thematic status of the pronoun: the PP is in both cases considered given information, and when it is preposed, this will result in the interpretation of the rest of the sentence, including the pronoun, as new information. When the PP is postposed, however, the pronoun in initial position, which has the status of unmarked theme, will naturally be considered given information.

(211) a.  In *Leslie's* home town, *she* is still considered a good actress.

b.  Full NP:    $+1$                    Pronoun:     $0$

$$\frac{-1 \ (\text{given})}{.\ 0}$$

$$\frac{\begin{array}{l} -1 \ (\text{theme}) \\ +1 \ (\text{new}) \end{array}}{0}$$

(212) a.*She* is still considered a good actress in *Leslie's* home town.

b.  Pronoun:    $0$                    Full NP:    $+1$

$$\frac{\begin{array}{l} -1 \ (\text{theme}) \\ -1 \ (\text{given}) \end{array}}{-2}$$

$$\frac{-1 \ (\text{given})}{0}$$

## 5.3   *The Wider Explanatory Power of the Pragmatic Theory*

### 5.3.1   *Coordinate Structures*

Anaphora in coordinate structures is a phenomenon that a syntactic approach cannot account for (see section 3.2.3). In the present analysis the acceptability versus unacceptability of sentences like (213) and (214) is simply due to the interaction of two pragmatic principles, the Super-principle and Principle B. As will be recalled, the latter principle says that the referent of a pronoun must be known from the immediate context, usually previous discourse.

(213)   *Leslie* wanted to buy the dress, but *she* didn't have the money.

(214)   *\*She* wanted to buy the dress, but *Leslie* didn't have the money.

Sentence (213) follows Principle B, while this principle is violated in (214). It is, however, the violation of the Super-principle which blocks coreference in (214); although both NPs are themes in their respective clauses, the first theme in a coordinate structure must be considered more thematic than the second. In terms of scalar values, then, the assignment of negative points on the scale to the second NP must result in the assignment of twice this value to the first NP. The first NP will thus have a value of -2, and the scalar analysis of the above sentences will look like (215) and (216) respectively:

(215) Full NP:     +1                 Pronoun:     0
                   $\underline{-2 \text{ (theme)}}$              $\underline{-1 \text{ (theme)}}$
                   $-1$                           $-1$

(216) Pronoun:     0                   Full NP:     +1
                   $\underline{-2 \text{ (theme)}}$              $\underline{-1 \text{ (theme)}}$
                   $-2$                           0

In most coordinate structures the full NP precedes its coreferring pronoun, which is in accordance with all the pragmatic principles stated in Chapter 4. There are certain very puzzling examples, however, where the full NP follows the pronoun, and the sentence is nevertheless grammatical with co-reference. Consider for example the following sentence:

(217) *She* has the whole world in front of her, and yet *Leslie* simply sits at home.

A sentence like (217) has a very special information value. The first part of it can be said to express some kind of irritation or criticism on the part of the speaker. This may then be somehow understood as the speaker's argument and thus as new information, as compared to the second part of the sentence which is most likely known or given information. In terms of scalar values, therefore, such a sentence can be given the following interpretation:

(218) Pronoun:     0                   Full NP:     +1
                   $-2$ (theme)                    $-1$ (theme)
                   $\underline{+1 \text{ (new)}}$                $\underline{-1 \text{ (given)}}$
                   $-1$                           $-1$

### 5.3.2   *Indefinite NPs*

In a syntactic approach to anaphora the coreference options of pronouns and indefinite NPs cannot be accounted for by the same principle that restricts coreference between pronouns and definite NPs, a fact which was criticized in section 3.2.5. In the present section I will try to show that the anaphora rule in my pragmatic approach can in fact account for both cases. As will be recalled, this rule is now formulated as the Super-principle, which briefly states that a pronoun may not be more thematic than the full NP from which it picks up its reference. The difference between definite and indefinite NPs, I will argue, lies simply in the thematic value that is attributed to the NPs at the outset of the analysis; while a definite NP starts out at $+1$, an extra point must be given for indefiniteness, so that an indefinite NP really starts out at $+2$. That this system would in fact work is demonstrated in the following examples, where definite and indefinite NPs are compared:

(219) a.   Before *he* knew it, *Peter* had been arrested.[55]

     b.   Pronoun:     0                Full NP:    $+1$

                                                     $-1$   (theme)

                       ‾‾‾‾‾‾‾‾‾‾                   ‾‾‾‾‾‾‾

                          0                               0

(220) a. *Before *he* knew it, *a man* had been arrested.

     b.   Pronoun:     0                Full NP:    $+2$

                                                     $-1$   (theme)

                       ‾‾‾‾‾‾‾‾‾‾                   ‾‾‾‾‾‾‾

                          0                               $+1$

(221) a.   The man who kissed *her* liked *Leslie*.

     b.   Pronoun:     0                Full NP:    $+1$

                                                     $+1$   (rheme)

               $+1$   (new)                   $-1$   (given)

               ‾‾‾‾‾‾‾‾‾‾‾                  ‾‾‾‾‾‾‾

                 $+1$                              $+1$

(222) a. *The man who kissed *her* liked *a woman*.

     b.   Pronoun:     0                Full NP:    $+2$

                                                     $+1$   (rheme)

               $+1$   (new)                   $-1$   (given)

               ‾‾‾‾‾‾‾‾‾‾‾                  ‾‾‾‾‾‾‾

                 $+1$                              $+2$

In both (219) and (221), the pronoun and the full (definite) NP have equal values on the scale in terms of thematicity. When the definite NP is replaced by an indefinite NP, therefore, as in (220) and (222), this balance is lost, with the result that the pronoun is now more thematic than the full NP. The Super-principle then rules that the pronoun may not pick up its reference from this NP, and the sentences are thus unacceptable with coreference.

Since there is such a discrepancy in thematic values between a pronoun and an indefinite NP already at the outset of the analysis, the latter seems always to have to precede the former for coreference to be possible. In earlier versions of transformational-generative grammar it was also assumed, e.g. by Postal (1970), that with indefinite NPs any kind of backwards pronominalization was blocked. There are certain cases, however, where the opposite order of the two NPs is possible. One example of this is when the pronoun occurs in a structure that clearly expresses new information, e.g. in a cleft sentence. The following sentence could therefore be acceptable in the appropriate situation:

(223) a. It was only to tease *him* that the girls gave *a man* at the party a kiss.

b. Pronoun:     0                         Full NP:   +2
$$\frac{+1 \text{ (new)}}{+1}$$                    $$\frac{-1 \text{ (given)}}{+1}$$

# 6
# Conclusion

## 6.0 *General Remarks*

This concluding chapter consists of five different sections. Firstly, I will give a summary of the analysis of anaphoric relations that has been presented in this thesis, and secondly, I will discuss some of the aspects of anaphora that this theory seems to run into difficulties with. Thirdly, an attempt will be made to see this analysis in a wider perspective, and the type of framework it could be integrated into will be considered. In the fourth section, this analysis will also be related to a theory of processing and compared with the discussion of this in Reinhart (1983b). Finally, some topics for further research will be suggested.

## 6.1 *Summary of the Theory*

The present discussion of anaphora took as its point of departure the treatment of this linguistic phenomenon in modern syntactic frameworks. Although in the most recent version of generative grammar this is quite elegantly described in terms of the notion of c-command (Reinhart (1976)), this analysis was shown to be both theoretically and empirically unsatisfactory.

My hypothesis at the outset of this research was that it should be possible to set up certain pragmatic principles that could be found to govern all the co-reference options of NPs in sentences. Some pragmatic analyses of this phenomenon had been attempted (e.g. Kuno 1972a, 1972b, 1975, Bickerton 1975 and Bolinger 1979), but since these basically considered only one aspect of pragmatics, namely the distinction between given and new information (or presupposition/assertion in Bickerton's framework and theme/rheme in Bolinger's analysis), these approaches to anaphora were not found to be adequate either.

I therefore proceeded to construct a theory of anaphora that took account of three pragmatic factors: the linear order of the two NPs in terms of theme/

rheme structure, the information value (given/new) of these NPs, and finally the question of whether the NP could carry focus. A scalar system was constructed, and the NPs of a sentence were given points on this scale according to the amount of *thematicity* (based on the three factors above) they carried. This scalar system of thematicity was founded on certain well-known pragmatic principles, such as the principle of Functional Sentence Perspective (FSP) of Czech linguistics. The anaphora rule in the present theory was defined as a Super-principle, formulated in (159) above, which briefly said that a pronoun could not be more thematic than a full NP in the same sentence from which it picked up its reference. The interaction of the Super-principle and the scalar system was found to make correct predictions for the acceptability of sentences in an overwhelming majority of cases (in Chapter 5).

## 6.2   *Remaining Problems*

Despite the above statement, the present analysis of anaphora does not seem to be able to account for all coreference facts in sentences with pronouns and full NPs. There are certain sentences that resist an analysis in terms of scalar values, and this appears to be due to a theoretical weakness of the analysis that is related to the distinction between given and new information.

The criterion for the assignment of values to NPs as given or new information is not as clear as could be desired in the present state of the theory. Sometimes these values are assigned on the basis of previous discourse, in other cases this assignment is simply based on linear order (according to the principle of FSP), while in some further cases the assignment of values is due to the interpretation of a certain syntactic construction. This fact is not necessarily an argument against my theory, but it could cause a problem if the three criteria are not compatible with each other. In such a case, which one would override the others?

It is possible that the answer to this question lies in a refinement of the scalar system, and that the distinction given/new should be discarded and replaced by a tripartite system which takes account of *discourse context*, *linear order* (irrespective of theme/rheme relations) as well as the interpretation of certain *syntactic constructions*.

A possible refinement of the theory was also alluded to above (see section 4.2.4.5). It was there mentioned that the theory may need to distinguish between more elaborate structures such as embedded themes and embedded rhemes. This could be especially relevant since most of the sentences discussed in this thesis involve structures that can be characterized as complex sentences, i.e they consist of both main and subordinate (embedded) clauses. A final pragmatic aspect that should possibly be taken account of is *specificity* (see note 55), as this is closely related to and partly interacts with definiteness. However, as most of the sentences that are common in recent analyses of anaphora can in fact be analyzed in terms of a more simplified system, the scope of this thesis has been limited to the three pragmatic aspects of theme/rheme, given/new and focus structure.

The sentences that pose a problem for this theory of anaphora are of the type that Ross (1969) used to argue for the cyclicity of Pronominalization. In the following sentences, he claimed, pronominalization could go both forwards and backwards:

(224) That *Peter* was unpopular didn't disturb *him*.

(225) That *he* was unpopular didn't disturb *Peter*.

Sentence (224) can easily be accounted for by the scalar system of thematicity, as shown in (226b) below: the pronoun is in rheme position and therefore also considered new information (with normal intonation). It is thus more rhematic than the full NP, and coreference is possible. If the full NP is stressed, however, this causes a change in the interpretation of these NPs. The full NP must now also be considered new information, and it thereby becomes more rhematic than the pronoun. The Super-principle is thus violated, and coreference is blocked in (226c).

(226) a.  That *Peter* was unpopular didn't disturb *him*.

    b.  Full NP:  +1           Pronoun:   0

$$
\begin{array}{ll}
\text{Full NP:} \quad +1 & \text{Pronoun:} \quad 0 \\
 & +1 \ \text{(rheme)} \\
\underline{-1 \ \text{(given)}} & \underline{+1 \ \text{(new)}} \\
\quad\; 0 & +2
\end{array}
$$

    c.*That *Péter* was unpopular didn't disturb *him*.

$$
\begin{array}{ll}
\text{d. Full NP:} \quad +1 \ \text{(new)} & \text{Pronoun:} \\
\underline{+1 \ \text{(focus)}} & \\
\quad\; +3 & \qquad\quad +2
\end{array}
$$

A sentence like (225) is more problematic for this analysis, however. The full NP is in rheme position, and if the values for given and new information are assigned according to linear order, as in (226), the result is a value of +3 for the full NP and −1 for the pronoun. Since the pronoun is more thematic here, the sentence should be unacceptable with coreference, which, of course, it is not:

(227) a. That *he* was unpopular didn't disturb *Peter*.

b. Pronoun:    0                    Full NP:   +1
                                               +1  (rheme)
         −1  (given)                           +1  (new)
         ──────────                            ──────────
            −1                                   +3

An explanation for this could be sought in the effect of intonation in such a sentence. If the final NP is stressed (which I have previously argued to be the normal intonation pattern here), it either does not corefer with the pronoun or it has contrastive function:

(228) a.*That *he* was unpopular didn't disturb *Pêter*.

b. That *he* was unpopular didn't disturb *Peter*, but it disturbed everybody else in his family.

This suggests that for the two NPs to corefer, the full NP must be considered given information. This approach would give the following result, which at first sight seems to solve the problem, since the two NPs have equal values:

(229) a. That *he* was unpopular didn't disturb *Peter*.

b. Pronoun:    0                    Full NP:   +1
                                               +1  (rheme)
         +1  (new)                            −1  (given)
         ──────────                            ──────────
            +1                                   +1

However, this solution does not explain why the sentence is still acceptable (in the contrastive reading) when the full NP carries stress (as in 228b). In this case, the full NP should be assigned one extra point on the scale as focus, which would increase its value to +2. It would then be more rhematic than the pronoun, and the Super-principle would interpret the two NPs as non-coreferential. This dismaying result suggests that there is more to be said about contrastiveness and the relationship between this aspect of pragmatics and the given/new distinction than is possible in the present state of the theory.

A second set of sentences which cause some difficulties with regard to the scalar system are also taken from Ross (1969). These are sentences which, according to the Standard Theory, are produced by an interaction of the transformations Pronominalization and EQUI (NP Deletion). In this case, only backwards pronominalization is possible:

(230) *Realizing that *Peter* was unpopular didn't disturb *him*.

(231)  Realizing that *he* was unpopular didn't disturb *Peter*.

Again, the former of the two sentences allows a scalar analysis. The pronoun is the rheme of the sentence, but since it cannot carry stress (without causing a change in coreference options), it must be considered given information. It is therefore more thematic than the full NP, and accordingly, the sentence is considered unacceptable with coreference. If the pronoun is stressed, however, it must be interpreted as new information, and the analysis in (232d) correctly predicts the sentence to be acceptable.

(232) a.*Realizing that *Peter* was unpopular didn't disturb *him*.

b.  Full NP:    +1              Pronoun:      0
                                             +1  (rheme)
            +1  (new)                        -1  (given)
            ————————                         ————————
             +2                               0

c.  Realizing that *Peter* was unpopular didn't disturb *hím*.

d.  Full NP:                    Pronoun:     +1  (focus)
                                             +1  (new)
                                             ————————
             +2                               +3

Sentence (231) poses a similar problem as (229) above. As long as only the distinctions theme/rheme and given/new are considered, the scalar analysis is compatible with the acceptability of the sentence. But this analysis is not able to explain why the sentence is still acceptable when the full NP carries contrastive stress, as in (233c), and should, according to the rules for focus assignment, be added one more point.

(233) a. Realizing that *he* was unpopular didn't disturb *Peter*.

b. Pronoun:     0              Full NP:     +1
                                            +1 (rheme)
                +1 (new)                    −1 (given)
                —————                       —————
                +1                          +1

c. Realizing that *he* was unpopular didn't disturb *Péter*.

d. Pronoun:                    Full NP:     +1 (focus)
                                            +1 (new)
                                            —————
                +1                          +4

It is arguable that the role of syntax should be taken into account in the analysis of sentences like the above. In underlying structure there is supposedly a pronoun present as the subject of the initial verb. In a pragmatic analysis this could also simply be regarded as a psychological or logical subject which for syntactic reasons happens not to be realized in the phonetic output. If this subject were to be considered, one could claim that the acceptability of sentences like (230) and (231) should be dependent on the analysis that they would be subject to if this underlying pronoun were present, as in (234) and (235) below. The unacceptability of (230) would then not be due to the fact that the full NP cannot corefer with the following pronoun, but rather that it cannot corefer with the one that precedes.

(234) *\*He* realized that *Peter* was unpopular.

(235) *He* realized that *he* was unpopular.

## 6.3 *The Framework*

The theory that has been outlined in this thesis is based on pragmatic principles and could therefore easily be incorporated into a functional framework, e.g. that of the Prague linguists. The coreference options of pronouns and full NPs have been found to be dependent on pragmatic factors such as theme/rheme and given/new, both of which are well-known notions in pragmatic theories.

The question is therefore whether the results of the present analysis are compatible with the syntactic theory of Government and Binding. If one considers the treatment of anaphora in this framework, the answer must certainly be no, as there is a sharp contrast between the two analyses; while the GB framework considers anaphora strictly to be a matter of syntax and therefore formalizable as a structural constraint, the functional approach that has been taken in this thesis claims that pragmatic principles are solely responsible for the coreference options of full NPs and pronouns.

As pragmatics is an area of language and linguistics that pure syntacticians do not consider to be a part of grammar, it seems impossible to try to incorporate the present theory into a syntactic framework. But since the most recent version of generative syntax postulates a modular theory of language, there should not à priori be anything preventing the addition of yet another module, e.g. a pragmatic component. This could in the syntactic model (represented in (99) above) be placed after the semantic component of Logical Form. The anaphora rule, now formulated as the Super-principle in (159), would then be operating in the pragmatic component and there interpret the thematicity of the various NPs and their coreference options. Seen in this perspective, the present account of anaphora *is* in fact compatible with the Government and Binding framework as a general theory, although it is not, of course, in concord with the analysis of anaphora in this theory.

## 6.4  *A Theory of Processing*

Reinhart (1983b) tries to find evidence in a theory of processing for her formulation of the anaphora constraint in terms of c-command, and she argues that if 'the same conditions restrict the operation of unrelated rules at various levels, this suggests that they may reflect general properties of the processing ability of the mind' (p. 202). In this perspective, the anaphora rule is simply seen as 'a particular case of more general conditions restricting the operation of semantic-interpretation [ as well as syntactic, MRW] rules' (p.181).

Several linguists have tried to explain how speakers perceive and process an acoustic input, but there does not as yet exist a widely accepted theory of processing. The main question concerns the processing units, i.e. how big are the linguistic 'chunks' that are processed and interpreted simultaneously? The assumption is that linguistic information is kept in the short-term memory until a 'closure' is reached at the end of the unit. Some linguists, e.g. Fodor, Bever and Garrett (1974), and Bever (1975), argue that the processing unit is the clause, while others, e.g. Kimball (1973), claim that processing takes place after the rightmost element of a constituent has been reached. Reinhart takes the latter approach and finds that this constituent-processing theory correlates with her postulation of certain domain conditions (DCs) based on c-commmand, which are supposed to restrict all rules.

Since the notion of c-command as well as the syntactic structures that it is supposed to restrict are fairly complex, I assume that the conditions must be considered universal and therefore built into the minds of humans already at birth (or developed in early childhood). But as very little is known about the human brain as well as the structure of the majority of natural languages, I find it a fairly premature assumption. (So far it has seemed quite complicated to find any universals in language that can survive a closer investigation.) Another major problem of this approach is of course that c-command has been found not to work in all cases, and that there would be a considerable number of exceptions that would have to be memorized by speakers anyway.

I will therefore suggest the following very simple processing strategy for pronouns in English: whenever a speaker of a language hears a pronoun, he/she will start searching for a referent, either in deictic or in linguistic context. If there is no deictic context, the antecedent will first be searched for in previous discourse, where there does not seem to be a statable restriction on how far back one can go (although memory, of course, plays an important role here). If no possible antecedent for the pronoun can be found in previous discourse, the pronoun will be 'held' in the short-term memory until an NP has been reached which can determine the reference of this pronoun. The strategy on the part of the hearer/reader can be formulated as follows:

(236) Whenever you hear/see a pronoun:

   A. Search in previous discourse for an antecedent which agrees with the pronoun in gender and number.

   B. Do not 'close' the unit of interpretation until a possible antecedent has been reached.

One could also in this connection ask how speakers process the question of whether the pronoun can in fact corefer with the full NP? Although I do not wish to claim that the scalar system that I have postulated in this thesis has any psychological reality, there must be, in addition to the Super-principle, a way for speakers to determine the thematicity of NPs, taking account of (at least) the three factors found to be significant for this. All this should be material simple enough to be learned, so no universal claim has to be made. These pragmatic aspects should also be unproblematic to process, since they are all available in the surface form of the sentences.

## 6.5  *Further Research*

As shown in section 6.2, there are certain sentences that are not analyzable in
the present theory of anaphora. This does not, I would like to argue, prove that
this approach to the problem of anaphoric relations is totally fallacious and
should therefore be rejected, but rather that it is still in an incomplete state.
The theory therefore needs development and refinement in the way indicated
in 6.2; i.e. a closer investigation of pragmatic aspects such as contrastiveness,
specificity, discourse context etc. is called for.

Such an investigation could take a corpus analysis as its point of departure.
It is important to examine 'real' language and find out what speakers actually
say and write, and it is possible that when one no longer deals with 'constructed' sentences, one would find the constraints to be inadequate in many
respects. (I suspect that this would affect a syntactic analysis to a greater
extent.) The fact that sentences would not be regarded in isolation would be
another advantage of a corpus analysis, as context obviously plays an important role in the coreference options of NPs.

This would enable us to investigate the question of grammaticality versus
acceptability. While syntacticians claim that sentences are either grammatical
or ungrammatical, I have argued that sentences can be more or less acceptable
depending on pragmatic plausibility. This could be related to the 'anaphora
hierarchy' set up by Lakoff (1968), which, he claims, mirrors the
acceptability versus unacceptability of sentences. This hierarchy distinguishes between four types of NPs corresponding to the conditions under
which these NPs can serve as anaphoric expressions: proper names, definite
descriptions, epithets and pronouns. These NPs are assigned values on a scale
(in the above order), and Lakoff predicts that 'an NP with a lower number in
the hierarchy may be an antecedent of an NP with a higher number, but not
vice versa' (p. 296). It would be interesting to try to integrate Lakoff's theory
into the scalar system presented in this thesis and investigate to what extent the
two can be said to correlate.

An investigation of this type would also have to explore various types of
language and attempt to find answers to several questions, e.g. what is the
percentage of sentences that can be accounted for by c-command and how
many can be explained in terms of the Super-principle, when are these constraints disregarded by speakers (if ever) and in what contexts, and how fre-
quent are sentences that are crucial for the two analyses, e.g. sentences with
preposed PPs? The question of processing mentioned in the previous section
could also inspire much research that would test the way speakers actually
process the reference of NPs. Finally, it would be interesting to find if there is

a sociolinguistic aspect related to the use and non-use of pronouns as indicated by Bernstein (1970) (see note 36).

In conclusion, therefore, one is forced to admit that despite the massive amount of literature that has been devoted to anaphora in various frameworks in recent years, there are still many unanswered questions in this area, and it is likely that this topic will continue to interest linguists for many years to come. The pragmatic analysis presented in this thesis has attempted to solve some of the problems connected with syntactic approaches, and if further research is carried out as outlined above, my prediction is that one should be able to take considerable steps towards an answer to the mystery of anaphora.

# Notes

1. Italicized elements indicate coreference.

2. This sentence is asterisked, i.e. considered ungrammatical, only in the coreferential reading.

3. *t* stands for the trace left by the moved *wh*-element.

4. Note that this definition makes crucial reference to pragmatics, a fact that will be returned to later in this thesis.

5. Morphophonemic rules which assign the correct person, number, case etc. to the pronoun must apply between the two stages of the derivation shown in (9) and (10).

6. Note that Extraposition and Passive are both transformations that can be said to have pragmatic function (see section 5.2.2).

7. Deictic pronouns are pronouns that can be used without a linguistic antecedent in contexts where it is understood—either by pointing or simply by physical presence—who or what the referent of the pronoun is. An example is the situation where two people walk along a road and meet a man that one of them says hello to. It is then perfectly natural for the other to utter the following sentence:

    (i)  Did you know *him*?

    although no linguistic reference to this person has been made in the previous discourse.

8. These terms are due to Ross (1969).

9. These are simplified trees. More elaborate structures with $\bar{\text{S}}$, COMP etc. will be used only when necessary. The indices indicate coreferential elements.

10. (33c), as well as the underlying structure in (33a), will of course be considered ungrammatical with coreference as a surface structure.

11. It will be pointed out at a later stage in this thesis (section 3.2) that this is not quite so simple after all.

12. Although I naturally accept the importance of structural relations and agree that the notion of c-command is fundamental in syntactic analyses, I will later try to show that linear order plays a crucial role pragmatically.

13. The reason why 'Case' is capitalized here is the fact that the Government and Binding framework uses this word in a technical sense to refer to abstract 'Case', not its morphological realization.

14. It should be noted that this is in accordance with other aspects of the theory; deep structures are for example no longer produced by phrase structure rules, but trees are just randomly constructed in the base, subject to certain well-formedness conditions.

15. The possible coreference of the two NPs in sentences like (57) has also been called 'pragmatic coreference' by Partee (1978), 'coreference with no dependency' by Evans (1980), and 'accidental coreference' by Lasnik (1976).

16. Chomsky (1980) actually needs the original definition of c-command to formulate his opacity constraint.

17. Examples of these three tests are:

   *though*-Movement

   (i) a.   Find scratches in Peter's picture though she did, Leslie...

   b. *Find scratches though she did in Peter's picture, Leslie...

   *wh*-Movement

   (ii) a. *In Peter's picture, who found scratches?

   b.   In Peter's picture, who is wearing a blue dress?

   VP Preposing

   (iii) a.   They wanted her to find a scratch in Peter's picture, and find a scratch in his picture she did.

   b. *They wanted her to find a scratch in Peter's picture, and find a scratch she did in his picture.

18. Sentence (70b) would of course be grammatical if Peter's picture actually depicted Leslie finding scratches, in which case, however, the PP would be sentential.

19. This is the most recent formulation of Subjacency which occurs at various places in the EST/GB literature. The notion originated in Chomsky (1973).

20. This claim is not based on any systematic research, but simply on the observation of the general reaction to example sentences with anaphora when presented to native speakers in a classroom situation, more specifically in Professor Sandra Chung's Syntax course given at the University of California, San Diego, during the Winter quarter of 1984. It is also a well-known fact that linguists often disagree on the grammaticality of certain constructions depending on whether it 'fits' their theory or not. For example, a structure like the following is considered ungrammatical by Ross (1969), but grammatical by Langacker (1969):

   (i)   Girls who *he* has dated like *Peter*.

21. Reinhart relies heavily on Williams's (1974) analysis of PPs, which claims, among other things, that an instrumental PP (as in (91)) must obligatorily originate under the VP.

22. Again, I have no statistical material to rely on, but the fact that quite a few people accept these sentences seems to support my hypothesis that pragmatic plausibility is stronger than syntactic structure.

23. Given by Professor Sandra Chung at University of California, San Diego, in the Spring quarter of 1984.

24. The data discussed in this section have been noted by several people, but have not, to my knowledge at least, been published anywhere. The material was presented to me as a problem set to be solved in Professor Chung's syntax class in the Winter quarter of 1984.

25. D-structures and S-structures in this Government and Binding framework are not identical to the deep and surface structures of the Standard Theory. The difference mainly concerns the S-structures, which are now enriched and thus more abstract syntactic trees. Empty elements and traces are still present at S-structure, and it is therefore possible at this point to trace the derivational history of a sentence. The actual phonetic form of the sentence is the output of the phonological component.

26. This type of sentence is identical in structure to those referred to in section 3.1.2.

27. In the search for extremely general formulations of various rules and principles in the Government and Binding framework, it has recently been suggested by Lasnik and Saito (1984) that the transformation 'Move $\alpha$' should be replaced by an even more general rule, 'Affect $\alpha$', which would include not only movement rules, but deletion rules as well.

28. In Chapter 5.

29. This is possibly also the reason for the great vacillation in grammaticality judgements.

30. Kuno makes a distinction between four types of semantic interpretation in language: theme, contrast, exhaustive listing and neutral description. This difference, he claims, manifests itself both in phonology and syntax. An example of the relevance of this distinction can be illustrated by the four different meanings of the following sentence:

    (i)   Alexander kissed Mary.

          a. [theme]: 'Speaking of Alexander, he kissed Mary.'
          b. [contrast]: 'As for Alexander, he kissed Mary', as in *Alexander kissed Mary, but Bill didn't*.
          c. [exhaustive listing]: 'It was Alexander who kissed Mary', as in *Who kissed Mary? (Only) Alexander kissed Mary*.
          d. [neutral description]: 'It happened that Alexander kissed Mary', as in *What happened next? Alexander kissed Mary*. (Kuno 1972b, p. 297).

31. Carden cites the following reference for this sentence: Letter, *New York Times*, 28 Jan, 1977.

32. Bolinger's definition of *theme* is similar to that of Firbas in that it is considered to be the element conveying given or old information. The PP in (139) conveys given information, but it is doubtful whether Bolinger would actually characterize a final PP as the theme of the sentence.

33. See definition of *rhematic* below.

34. It has been claimed (for example by the founder of the Prague school, V. Mathesius) that English does not have enough syntactic means to put all sentences in the unmarked *theme-transition-rheme* sequence, and that it is thus insusceptible to the principle of FSP. Firbas (1966), however, argues convincingly that although it might be true that many sentences of English disobey this principle, it is also clear that many syntactic devices have exactly the function of creating a *theme-rheme* order, and he thus concludes that English *is* in fact susceptible to FSP, but perhaps to a lesser degree than certain other languages, e.g. Czech.

35. The term *theme* is here used in a non-technical sense.

36. It seems to be a common mistake among native and non-native speakers alike to use pronouns in situations where it is actually *not* clear who the referent is. This phenomenon is also an important aspect in Bernstein's (1970) famous, but controversial, distinction between restricted and elaborated code. He claims, among other things, that an important feature of the restricted code is an overuse of ambiguous pronouns.

37. Note that the acceptability of this sentence is dependent on the intonation—if the final NP were stressed, the sentence would be unacceptable.

38. It is possible that this restriction should be defined grammatically, i.e. in terms of *subject* instead of *unmarked theme*, since in the cases where one has a preposed marked theme, the same restriction holds:

      (i)    *An apple *she* had given to the man who *Leslie* liked.

I prefer to keep the formulation in (155), however, for two reasons. Firstly, the term subject cannot by itself be sufficient, as illustrated by (154) where one has an embedded subject, but the sentence is nevertheless acceptable. Secondly, I would like to claim that a sentence like (i) could be made acceptable (although, admittedly, it would be fairly unusual) with a change in intonation:

      (ii)   ?An apple *she* gave to the man *Leslie* liked.

It thus seems that the pronoun has to be both subject and unmarked theme for the restriction to hold. This solution is not undesirable, since it is common in languages for syntax and pragmatics to interact and reinforce each other.

39. I will later claim that this is in fact the most normal intonation pattern here. It should also be noted, as has been pointed out to me by Gjert Kristoffersen, that this sentence may actually be acceptable with coreference in a contrastive reading. The problem of contrastiveness will be discussed in section 6.2.

40. The term *thematic* is again used in the sense defined in 4.2.3.6 above.

41. There is of course a fourth possibility, namely the case where, with normal intonation, the pronoun is more thematic than the full NP, but where the addition of stress to the *pronoun* makes the two NPs equal in strength and coreference possible. I have, however, not been able to find an example of this, although (i) may be a possible candidate:

      (i)   a.*In *Peter's* home town, *he* spent most of his life.

b. Full NP:   +1                   Pronoun:  0

| b. Full NP: | | Pronoun: | |
|---|---|---|---|
| +1 | | 0 | |
| | | $-1$ | (theme) |
| $+1$ | (new) | $-1$ | (given) |
| $+2$ | | $-2$ | |

c. In *Peter's* home town, $\widehat{he}$ spent most of his life.

| d. Full NP: | | Pronoun: | |
|---|---|---|---|
| +1 | | 0 | |
| | | $-1$ | (theme) |
| | | $+1$ | (focus) |
| $-1$ | (given) | $+1$ | (new) |
| $0$ | | $+1$ | |

In (i), the stress shift causes a change in the information structure of the sentence, i.e. in the distribution of given and new information, as well as in the stressed element constituting the theme. See Chapter 5 for more discussion on this type of sentence.

42. Unlike Langacker and other syntacticians, I would like to argue that this sentence is in fact unacceptable with normal intonation, which assigns end-focus to the final NP. The sentence is therefore acceptable only when the stress has been shifted to the verb (i.e. when the transition element is focused), a change which also alters the given/new relationship. The result of such a change is given in (170c).

43. It should be noted that the definition of *given* and *new* information in these cases does not necessarily refer to the question of whether or not the NP has been mentioned in previous discourse. Rather, a PP in initial position which is considered to convey given information has the effect of 'setting the scene' for the rest of the sentence (this expression has been used by other pragmaticians for various linguistic phenomena and by Kuno (1975) for this particular one). An initial PP conveying new information, on the other hand, is considered an important part of the rest of the sentence that simply happens to be preposed for prominence. The difference between these two elements can thus be said to be the same as the difference between marked and unmarked themes.

44. It is possible that the assignment of given and new information should also be switched here, but this would merely increase the discrepancy in values in the desired direction, and strengthen the unacceptability of the result.

45. Note that in this sentence it is crucial that the interpretation of given and new information is different from that of the corresponding sentence in (174a); in (176) the full NP has to be considered given, while the pronoun must be considered new information. This is in accordance with the interpretation of the PP, which in this case must be understood as 'setting the scene' for the rest of the sentence.

46. Note that unlike its counterpart, (175), which is unacceptable when the full NP carries stress, (177c) is fine with coreference. In the present system this can be accounted for by the absence in the latter case of the point on the minus side of the scale that is attributed to the theme. Both sentences, however, are fairly marginal, and their acceptability, I am sure, could be a matter of much discussion.

47. This sentence, (180e), is very dubious as to its acceptability. I am inclined to accept it, but only in the reading where the pronoun must be interpreted as new information. The difference between the two possible interpretations becomes clear when one compares two different contexts for it:

(i)   a. They are known to be difficult, but at least they let $\overset{\frown}{him}$ spend most of his life in *Peter's* home town.

    b. Pronoun:    0                  Full NP: +1

| | |
|---|---|
| +1 (focus) | |
| +1 (new) | −1 (given) |
| +2 | 0 |

(ii)  a.*Peter is known to be difficult, but at least they let $\overset{\frown}{him}$ spend most of his life in *Peter's* home town.

    b. Pronoun:    0                  Full NP: +1

| | |
|---|---|
| +1 (focus) | |
| −1 (given) | +1 (new) |
| 0 | +2 |

In (ii), the pronoun will be interpreted as picking up its reference from the full NP in the preceding clause. In addition to the Super-principle, principle D is also violated here, since it is unnecessary to reintroduce the full NP when it is clear who the referent is.

48. The following sentence provides us with a similar example. In this case the full NP is the rheme proper.

    (i)   a.*They locked *him* into the garage that they had built for *Peter*.

        b. Pronoun:    0                  Full NP: +1

| | |
|---|---|
| | +1 (rheme) |
| −1 (given) | +1 (new) |
| −1 | +3 |

With normal intonation (end-focus), this sentence is ungrammatical. If stress is shifted forwards to the verb, however, the sentence becomes more acceptable since this also changes the given/new relationship:

    (ii)  a. They locked *him* into the garage that they had $\overset{\frown}{built}$ for *Peter*.

        b. Pronoun:    0                  Full NP: +1

| | |
|---|---|
| | +1 (rheme) |
| +1 (new) | −1 (given) |
| +1 | +1 |

49. It is of course difficult to say which element is new and which is given in this sentence, since neither has been previously mentioned. Note, however, that the distinction between given and new information is not crucial to account for the unacceptability here and may well be disregarded.

50. It is actually unclear whether a syntactic analysis could account for the acceptability of this sentence, since a topicalized element is usually moved into COMP, and as illustrated by the structure of this sentence represented in the following syntactic tree, the pronoun c-commands the full NP, and a coreferential reading should be impossible.

(i)

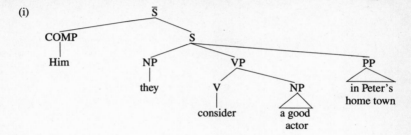

51. The newness of the pronoun in these sentences is actually superfluous here, since the position of the NPs in terms of theme/rheme is sufficient to account for the acceptability versus unacceptability of the sentences.

52. Here I use surface structure in the old sense of this term as it is conceived of in the framework of the Standard Theory of transformational-generative grammar. I am thus not referring to the more abstract S-structures of the Government and Binding theory, where traces and empty elements are actually still present in the syntactic tree.

53. The question of whether this takes place in the semantic component or in a special pragmatic component will be returned to in section 6.3.

54. Sentences like (200) and (202) will be discussed in section 6.2.

55. I have disregarded the distinction between given and new information in (219) and (220). This is partly because it is irrelevant to the point at issue, but also because it here involves one more aspect of the theory, namely the distinction between specific and non-specific NPs, which possibly should be integrated into the scalar system, but which I do not wish to go into in this thesis.

# Bibliography

*References*

Bernstein, B. (1970). 'A Sociolinguistic Approach to Socialization: with some reference to educability', in F. Williams (ed.), *Language and Poverty*, pp. 25-61, Markham, Chicago, Illinois.

Bever, T. G. (1975). 'Functional Explanations Require Independently Motivated Functional Theories', in R. E. Grossman et al. (eds.), pp. 580-609.

Bickerton, D. (1975). 'Some Assertions About Presuppositions About Pronominalization', in R. E. Grossman et al. (eds.), pp. 24-35.

Bolinger, D. (1977). *Meaning and Form*, Longman, London and New York.

Bolinger, D. (1979). 'Pronouns in Discourse', in T. Givon (ed.), *Discourse and Syntax, Syntax and Semantics*, pp. 289-309, Academic Press, New York.

Carden, G. (1982). 'Backwards Anaphora in Discourse Context', in *Journal of Linguistics*, vol. 18, pp. 361-387, Cambridge University Press, Cambridge, England.

Chafe, W. L. (1976). 'Givenness, Contrastiveness, Definiteness, Subjects, Topics, and Point of View', in C. N. Li (ed.), *Subject and Topic*, pp. 27-55, Academic Press, New York.

Chomsky, N. (1957). *Syntactic Structures*, Janua Lingarum, no. 4, Mouton and Co., The Hague.

Chomsky, N. (1965). *Aspects of the Theory of Syntax*, MIT Press, Cambridge, Massachusetts.

Chomsky, N. (1973). 'Conditions on Transformations', in S.R. Anderson and P. Kiparsky (eds.), *A Festschrift for Morris Halle*, pp. 232-286, Holt, Rinehart and Winston, Inc., New York.

Chomsky, N. (1976). 'Conditions on Rules of Grammar', in *Linguistic Analysis*, vol. 2, pp. 303-352, Elsevier Publishing Company, Inc., New York.

Chomsky, N. (1980). 'On Binding', in *Linguistic Inquiry*, vol. 11, pp. 1-46, MIT Press, Cambridge, Massachusetts.

Chomsky, N. (1981). *Lectures on Government and Binding*, Foris Publications, Dordrecht, Holland.

*The Concise Oxford Dictionary of Current English* (1966). Oxford University Press, London.

Evans, G. (1980). 'Pronouns', in *Linguistic Inquiry*, vol. 11, pp. 337-362, MIT Press, Cambridge, Massachusetts.

Firbas, J. (1966). 'Non-thematic Subjects in Contemporary English', in *Travaux Linguistiques de Prague*, vol. 2, pp. 339-356, Academia, Publishing House of the Czechoslovak Academy of Sciences, Prague, and University of Alabama Press.

Fodor, J. A., T. G. Bever and M. Garrett (1974). *The Psychology of Language*, McGraw Hill, New York.

Givon, T. (1979). Preface in T. Givon (ed.), *Discourse and Syntax, Syntax and Semantics*, vol. 12, pp. xiii-xx, Academic Press, New York.

Grice, H. P. (1975). 'Logic and Conversation', in P. Cole and J. L. Morgan (eds.), *Speech*

*Acts, Syntax and Semantics*, vol. 3, pp. 41-58, Academic Press, New York.

Grossman, R. E., L. J. San and T. Vance (eds.), (1975). *Papers from the Parasession on Functionalism*, Chicago Linguistic Society, Chicago, Illinois.

Halliday, M. A. K. (1970). 'Language Structure and Language Function', in J. Lyons (ed.), *New Horizons in Linguistics*, pp. 140-165, Penguin Books, Middlesex, England.

Hinds, J. (1982). 'Paragraph Structure and Pronominalization', in *Papers in Linguistics*, vol. 10, pp. 77-99, Linguistic Research, Inc., Edmonton, Alberta.

Jackendoff, R. S. (1972). *Semantic Interpretation in Generative Grammar*, MIT Press, Cambridge, Massachusetts.

Kimball, J. (1973). 'Seven Principles of Surface Structure Parsing in Natural Language', in *Cognition*, vol. 2, pp. 15-47, Mouton, The Hague.

Kuno, S. (1972a). 'Pronominalization, Reflexivization, and Direct Discourse', in *Linguistic Inquiry*, vol. 3, pp. 161-195, MIT Press, Cambridge, Massachusetts.

Kuno, S. (1972b). 'Functional Sentence Perspective: A Case Study from Japanese and English', in *Linguistic Inquiry*, vol. 3, pp. 269-320, MIT Press, Cambridge, Massachusetts.

Kuno, S. (1975). 'Three Perspectives in the Functional Approach to Syntax', in R. E. Grossman et al. (eds.), pp. 276-336.

Kuno, S. (1980). 'Functional Syntax', in E. A. Moravcsik and J. R. Wirth (eds.), *Current Approaches to Syntax, Syntax and Semantics*, vol. 13, pp. 117-135, Academic Press, New York.

Lakoff, G. (1968). 'Pronouns and Reference', in McCawley, J. D. (ed.), (1976), *Notes from the Linguistic Underground, Syntax and Semantics*, vol. 7, pp. 275-345, Academic Press, New York.

Langacker, R. W. (1969). 'Pronominalization and the Chain of Command', in D. A. Reibel and S. Schane (eds.), pp. 160-186.

Langacker, R. W. (1984). *Foundations of Cognitive Grammar*. To appear. Stanford University Press.

Lasnik, H. (1976). 'Remarks on Coreference', in *Linguistic Analysis*, vol. 2, pp. 1-22, Elsevier Publishing Company, Inc., New York.

Lasnik, H. and M. Saito (1984). 'On the Nature of Proper Government', in *Linguistic Inquiry*, vol. 15, pp. 235-289, MIT Press, Cambridge, Massachusetts.

Lees, R. B. and E. S. Klima (1963). 'Rules for English Pronominalization', in *Language*, vol. 39, pp. 17-28, LSA, Baltimore.

Magretta, W.R. (1977). *'Topic-Comment Structure and Linguistic Theory: A Functional Approach'*, Doctoral dissertation, University of Michigan, Xerox University Microfilms, Ann Arbor, Michigan.

McCawley, J. D. (1984). 'Anaphora and Notions of Command', ms.

Partee, B. (1978). 'Bound Variables and Other Anaphors', in D. Waltz (ed.), *Proceedings of TINLAP 2*, University of Illinois, Urbana, Illinois. (Quoted from Reinhart (1983b), no page reference given.)

Postal, P. (1971). *Cross-over Phenomena*, Holt, Rinehart, and Winston, Inc., New York.

Quirk, R. and S. Greenbaum (1973). *A University Grammar of English*, Longman, London.

Reibel, D. A. and S. Schane (eds.), (1969). *Modern Studies in English, Readings in Transformational Grammar*, Prentice-Hall, Inc., Englewood Cliffs, New Jersey.

Reinhart, T. (1976). *The Syntactic Domain of Anaphora*, Doctoral dissertation, MIT, Cambridge, Massachusetts.

Reinhart, T. (1981). 'Definite NP Anaphora and C-command Domains', in *Linguistic Inquiry*, vol. 12, pp. 605-635, MIT Press, Cambridge, Massachusetts.

Reinhart, T. (1983a). 'Coreference and Anaphora: A Restatement of the Anaphora Question', in *Linguistics and Philosophy*, vol. 6, pp. 47-88, D. Reidel Publishing Company, Dordrecht, Holland.

Reinhart, T. (1983b). *Anaphora and Semantic Interpretation*, Croom Helm, London and Canberra.

Ross, J. R. (1967). *Constraints on Variables in Syntax*, Doctoral dissertation, MIT, Cambridge, Massachusetts. Available from Indiana University Linguistics Club, Bloomington, Indiana.

Ross, J. R. (1969). 'The Cyclical Nature of English Pronominalization', in D. A. Reibel and S. Schane (eds.), pp. 187-200.

Williams, E. S. (1974). *Rule Ordering in Syntax*, Doctoral dissertation, MIT, Cambridge, Massachusetts.

*Sources Consulted but not Referred to*

Breivik, L. E. (1982). Lecture notes from course in Pragmatics, University of Tromsø, Spring semester 1982.

Breivik, L. E. (1983). *Existential There: A Synchronic and Diachronic Study*, Studia Anglistica Norvegica 2, Bergen.

Breivik, L. E. (1984). Review of A. Svoboda, 'Diatheme: A Study in Thematic Elements, their Contextual Ties, Thematic Progressions and Scene Progressions in a Text from Ælfric', in *Lingua*, vol. 64, pp. 380-386 North-Holland, Amsterdam.

Chung, S. (1984). Lecture notes from Syntax courses, Winter quarter 1984 and Spring quarter 1984 at University of California, San Diego.

Costa, R. (1975). 'A Functional Solution for Illogical Reflexives in Italian', in R. E. Grossman et al.(eds.), pp. 112-125.

Culicover, P. W. (1976). 'A Constraint on Coreferentiality', in *Foundations of Language*, vol. 14, pp. 109-118, D. Reidel Publishing Company, Dordrecht, Holland.

Daneš, F. (1974). *Papers on Functional Sentence Perspective*, Academia, Publishing House of the Czechoslovak Academy of Sciences, Prague, and Mouton, The Hague.

Dougherty, R. (1969). 'An Interpretive Theory of Pronominal Reference', in *Foundations of Language*, vol. 5, pp. 488-519, D. Reidel Publishing Company, Dordrecht, Holland.

Færch, C. (1975). 'Deictic NPs and Generative Pragmatics. A Possible Derivation of Deictic Nominal Expressions in Linguistics', in *Foundations of Language,* vol. 13, pp. 319- 348, D. Reidel Publishing Company, Dordrecht, Holland.

Gazdar, G. (1979). *Pragmatics: Implicature, Presupposition and Logical Form*, Academic Press, New York.

Gordon, D. and G. Lakoff (1975). 'Conversational Postulates', in P. Cole and J. L Morgan (eds.), *Speech Acts, Syntax and Semantics*, vol. 3, pp. 83-106, Academic Press, New York.

Grosu, A. (1975). 'A Plea for Greater Caution in Proposing Functional Explanations in Linguistics', in R. E. Grossman et al.(eds.), pp. 170-208.

Higginbotham, J. (1980). 'Pronouns and Bound Variables', in *Linguistic Inquiry*, vol. 11, pp. 679-708, MIT Press, Cambridge, Massachusetts.

Jacobs, R. and P. Rosenbaum (eds.), (1970). '*Readings in English Transformational Grammar*', Ginn and Co., Waltham, Massachusetts.

Karttunen, L. (1971). 'Definite Descriptions with Crossing Coreference. A Study of the Bach-Peters Paradox', in *Foundations of Language*, vol. 7, pp. 157-182, D. Reidel Publishing Company, Dordrecht, Holland.

Klima, E. (1983). Lecture notes from Syntax course, Fall quarter 1983 at University of California, San Diego.

Kreiman, K. J. and A. E. Oteda (eds.), (1980). *Papers from the Parasession on Pronouns and Anaphora*, Chicago Linguistic Society, Chicago, Illinois.

Kuno, S. (1975). 'Conditions for Verb Phrase Deletion', in *Foundations of Language*, vol. 13, pp. 161-175, D. Reidel Publishing Company, Dordrecht, Holland.

Kuroda, S.-Y. (1971). 'Two Remarks on Pronominalization', in *Foundations of Language*, vol.

7, pp. 183-198, D. Reidel Publishing Company, Dordrecht, Holland.

Lakoff, G. (1970). 'Pronominalization, Negation and the Analysis of Adverbs', in R. Jacobs and P. Rosenbaum (eds.), pp. 145-165.

Lyons, J. (1975). 'Deixis as a Source of Reference', in E. L. Keenan (ed.), *Formal Semantics of Natural Language*, pp. 61-83, Cambridge University Press, Cambridge, England.

McCawley, J. D. (1970). 'Where Do Noun Phrases Come From?', in R. Jacobs and P. Rosenbaum (eds.), pp. 166-183.

Morgan, J. L. (1975). 'Some Interactions of Syntax and Pragmatics', in P. Cole and J. L. Morgan (eds.), *Speech Acts, Syntax and Semantics*, vol. 3, pp. 289-303, Academic Press, New York.

Panhuis, D. G. J. (1982). *The Communicative Perspective in the Sentence: A Study of Latin Word Order*, John Benjamins Publishing Company, Amsterdam and Philadelphia.

Perlmutter, D. and S. Soames (1979). *Syntactic Argumentation and the Structure of English*, University of California Press, Berkeley and Los Angeles, California.

Postal, P. (1966). 'On 'So-called' Pronouns in English', in F. Dineen (ed.), *19th Monograph on Language and Linguistics*, Georgetown University Press, Washington D.C. Also published in D. A. Reibel and S. Schane (eds.), pp. 201-224.

Postal, P. (1970). 'On Coreferential Complement Subject Deletion', in *Linguistic Inquiry*, vol. 1, pp. 439-500, MIT Press, Cambridge, Massachusetts.

Postal, P. and J. R. Ross (1970). 'A Problem of Adverb Preposing', in *Linguistic Inquiry*, vol. 1, pp. 145-146, MIT Press, Cambridge, Massachusetts.

Postal, P. (1972). 'Some Further Limitations of Interpretive Theories of Anaphora', in *Linguistic Inquiry*, vol. 3, pp. 349-371, MIT Press, Cambridge, Massachusetts.

Reinhart, T. (1980). 'On the Position of Extraposed Clauses', in *Linguistic Inquiry*, vol. 11, pp. 621-624, MIT Press, Cambridge, Massachusetts.

Stockwell, R. P., P. Schachter and B. H. Partee (1973). *The Major Syntactic Structures of English*, Holt, Rinehart and Winston, Inc., New York.